Improving Community
Response to
Crime Victims

This book is dedicated to the millions of crime victims across the nation who are injured by violent crime each year. We hope that the information in this book—the eight-step Protocol Development Cycle—will help communities improve their response to these victims, and that all crime victims will receive the services they need and be treated with the dignity and respect they deserve.

Improving Community Response to Crime Victims

An
Eight-Step
Model for
Developing
Protocol

Anita B. Boles
John C. Patterson

 SAGE Publications
International Educational and Professional Publisher
Thousand Oaks   London   New Delhi

For information address:

SAGE Publications, Inc.
2455 Teller Road
Thousand Oaks, California 91320
E-mail: order@sagepub.com

SAGE Publications Ltd.
6 Bonhill Street
London EC2A 4PU
United Kingdom

SAGE Publications India Pvt. Ltd.
M-32 Market
Greater Kailash I
New Delhi 110 048 India

Printed in the United States of America

Library of Congress Cataloging-in-Publication Data

Boles, Anita B.
    Improving community response to crime victims: An eight-step
        model for developing protocol / Anita B. Boles, John C. Patterson.
            p.   cm.
    Includes bibliographical references (p.   ) and index.
    ISBN 0-8039-7244-X (cloth: acid-free paper)
    1. Victims of crimes—Services for—United States. 2. Victims of
        crimes—Legal status, laws, etc.—United States. I. Patterson,
        John C. II. Title.
    HV6250.3.U5B65 1997
    362.88—dc20
                                                                        96-25253

97 98 99 00 01 02 03 10 9 8 7 6 5 4 3 2 1

Acquiring Editor: C. Terry Hendrix
Editorial Assistant: Dale Grenfell
Production Editor: Diana E. Axelsen
Production Assistant: Karen Wiley
Typesetter/Designer: Christina Hill
Indexer: Jean Casalegno
Cover Designer: Candice Harman
Print Buyer: Anna Chin

Contents

Foreword

Twenty years ago, the typical response to an allegation of nonstranger child sexual abuse (assuming there was a response) might have involved separate and limited investigations by the police and child welfare agencies, an occasional medical evaluation by a physician with no training or experience dealing with child sexual assault, and perhaps haphazard counseling from someone who had no contact with any of the other professionals involved in the case. Criminal prosecutions were infrequent, testimony from children was rare, and most judges, lawyers, school professionals, probation officers, detectives, social workers, and other adults preferred to avoid such cases whenever possible. Too often, victimized children continued to live at risk and were left to suffer in silence.

As reports of these crimes mounted, and as awareness of the extent of child sexual abuse necessarily increased, they became impossible to ignore. Professionals began to realize the need for education and specialization. More cases were being dealt with in the civil and criminal justice systems, but the experience of victims was still less than satisfactory. Children were often confronted with a number of different adults from various agencies, each of whom would require another recounting of the abuse allegations. Police, social services, health care, and mental health agencies worked in isolation, each with its own job to do and each relying on traditional methods to accomplish that job. Cases would sometimes proceed on parallel tracks, with little or no interaction. Overworked professionals felt they had neither the time nor the need to coordinate their responses or to focus on the needs and reactions of victims. The results were often seemingly inconsistent statements causing problems regarding proof of the crime, or victims and families who became frustrated and unwilling to continue to cooperate. Something had to change.

And change it did. Professionals from diverse backgrounds began to exchange information informally and compare notes. They realized that there were benefits to working together, at least on some aspects of cases they had in common. They developed unofficial joint working arrangements. The results included less duplication of effort and more and better information available for all professionals to use in making decisions. Victims were less likely to face confusing and conflicting demands, and their input was more likely to be considered. But these informal efforts were dependent on the personalities and willingness of the individuals assigned to the cases, and they could completely disintegrate when personnel changed or supervisory policy shifted to new priorities. The need for more standard, formalized, interdisciplinary approaches became obvious, and the movement to institutionalize the multidisciplinary approach was underway.

For well over a decade now, multidisciplinary or interdisciplinary teams have been lauded as the best way to approach the investigation and prosecution of child sexual abuse cases. These teams, with public support from community leaders and agency heads, bring together key people involved in the cases who respond in a coordinated fashion and routinely exchange information. In the majority of situations, they work together to develop written guidelines (protocol) spelling out the ways in which agencies will interact in their response to defined cases of abuse.

Interagency coordination is also widely regarded as the key to successful resolution of a variety of other serious crimes—child homicide, serious physical abuse, adult sexual assault, serious juvenile offenses, and domestic violence. A number of state legislatures have mandated that cases involving offenses such as child abuse and child homicide be handled with a team approach. Thousands of professionals in communities across the United States have voluntarily joined together to develop and implement interagency protocol aimed at improving the handling of these complicated and difficult cases. Federal, state, and local resources have been devoted to supporting these efforts.

It would seem that with all this impetus supporting the concept of interagency coordination, the team approach should be relatively easy to get started, easy to keep going, and effective in meeting the needs of victims as well as those of the individual agencies. In fact, an effective interagency team approach to child abuse, sexual assault, domestic violence, or other serious crimes is very difficult to create and maintain. In the desire to comply with mandates requiring team efforts, or simply to improve case outcomes and respond better to the needs of victims, the effort often begins with a fanfare of meetings to declare good intentions. This is followed by a flurry of activity to reach written agreements. Much of the time, the result has been a document that sits on the shelf and is used for a short time or not at all, because it is too general, is unrelated to the reality of the situation in that community, or does not truly have the support of both policymakers and those in the trenches every day.

The true test of an interdisciplinary team is how its existence changes the experience of victims and affects the actions of its participants on every case they encounter. Although the type of crime the team is organized around may vary, some basic principles should guide communities who wish to create a successful coordinated system.

There currently exist a number of impressive efforts throughout the country. No two approaches are exactly alike. An efficacious protocol is tailored to the unique mix of agencies, resources, strengths, and weaknesses within each individual community. Professionals eager for improvement should not make the mistake of thinking that there is an effective shortcut to team creation and functioning by simply adopting another community's system. Although the ideas of others can often be used as a starting point to inspire, the end result must come from the combined hard work of those who will ultimately live with and apply the protocol that is developed. Those individuals must believe that it is relevant and responsive to their duties and circumstances.

Another critical factor is an understanding of and agreement about the goals of the team effort. That should be easy because, after all, everyone wants the same thing, don't they? The fact is that everyone does not always want the same thing. In child abuse cases, for example, prosecutors and law enforcement want to gather proof to ensure that abusers are held accountable and the community is protected; child protection agencies provide services to satisfy their mandate to reunify families whenever possible; and medical, mental health, and victim services professionals are interested in the well-being of victims, regardless of the technical proof of a crime. Failure of the team initiative can result from the inevitable disillusionment that follows a beginning in which everyone seems to be in apparent agreement that they all share the same goals.

Successful teams recognize that different members often have different goals, some of which conflict and compete. Rather than deny or disparage differences, they acknowledge and try to understand the various perspectives, and try to achieve resolutions that do the most to benefit victims and further the goals of all agencies. Where conflict cannot be avoided, agreements are aimed at minimizing it, with the interests of the victim providing a shared focus.

Although countless teams and protocol claim to have the best interests of victims as their linchpin, few efforts are truly "victim centered," in the sense that they do not rely on feedback from victims in their design, implementation, and evaluation. And yet, the victim is the one person all agencies have in common, and arguably the one with the most at stake. All agencies and professionals can ultimately support similar goals of protection, prevention, and healing. The best way to accomplish these goals is to make a commitment to being victim centered at the outset, with input from victims on a regular basis.

Undertaking the task of team building and protocol development is demanding. It can be threatening because it exposes what agencies currently do and requires accountability. Participants must learn to have an open mind and shed defensiveness as they engage in critical self-evaluation and constructive criticism of the role of others in the system. A serious hurdle is the fear of giving up control by agreeing to work as part of a team. It is imperative that everyone understand and agree up front that individual agencies retain full responsibility for decisions relating to their duties. The team does not "vote" or otherwise substitute its judgment for that of the police, prosecutor, physician, therapist, and so forth. Decisions made by those involved in an effective team process, however, should be better informed and receive greater support from victims as well as other agencies and professionals in the community.

An initially successful team approach toward one type of crime can lead to initiatives to institute similar teams for other crimes. Soon people who should be out investigating cases, consulting with victims, or otherwise working at specific tasks, are spending a majority of their time at various team meetings—the child abuse team, the child death review team, the sexual assault interagency council, the serious habitual juvenile offender team, and so on. Attendance at team meetings drops off as professionals decide they take up time that would be better spent doing "real" work. This is likely to occur when, as is frequently the case, necessary members of the team have responsibility in a number of areas such as child abuse, sexual assault, and domestic violence. The challenge then becomes how to integrate the different efforts into a more comprehensive team. Because these different kinds of cases almost never occur in isolation, and usually involve many overlapping areas, it makes sense to try to blend and unify such teams.

How can you tell when interdisciplinary teams and protocol are really successful? True success comes when those participating realize and accept that there never will be a point when they can say they have completed their work and accomplished their goals. Instead, they acknowledge that interdisciplinary efforts require an ongoing commitment to the process of assessment, evaluation, review, and revision.

The guidance offered in this book is based on many years of contact with a wide variety of professionals and communities. The authors have distilled the lessons learned from those experiences into a thoughtful and well-organized outline of steps and considerations for those who are serious about starting and maintaining an interagency team effort to respond to almost any type of serious interpersonal crime. Their commitment to victims is evident as the driving force throughout. They recognize that even small and relatively isolated communities have an impressive wealth of resources that can be marshalled to improve interagency coordination. Even communities with a tradition of good interdisciplinary cooperation can benefit from the process described here and enhance their response to victims, while achieving improved case outcomes.

Undertaking an interdisciplinary team approach is a daunting challenge, but one well worth the effort. It requires a significant investment of time and energy, coupled with a sincere desire to improve the system that exists for victims. Those who make the commitment will most certainly face occasional fatigue and frustration, but in the end will find the support and satisfaction that it takes to remain involved in the quest for justice for victims.

Patricia A. Toth, J.D.
Coupeville, Washington

Acknowledgments

The authors would like to acknowledge the National Victim Center for its contributions to this book and its dedication to improving community response to crime victims. We would also like to thank the U.S. Department of Justice, Office for Victims of Crime (OVC), for making community partnerships that enhance services to sexual assault victims a funding priority, as indicated by the original and continuation funds awarded to the National Victim Center for the grant project that inspired the development of the eight-step Protocol Development Cycle. A special acknowledgment to Melanie Smith, the OVC Project Monitor, whose support and contributions genuinely enhanced the success of the federal grant project and the original text, *Looking Back, Moving Forward: A Guidebook for Communities Responding to Sexual Assault*, on which this book is based. Patricia A. Toth, author of this book's Foreword and a key project staff on the federal grant, provided the benefit of her insights, which contributed greatly to the practical application of the Protocol Development Cycle, and offered steadfast encouragement for the completion of this book. We would like to recognize the efforts of the original test site—Snohomish County, Washington—and the two pilot interagency councils associated with the grant project—Pine Bluff, Arkansas, and Denver, Colorado—and congratulate them on their successes. A special note of appreciation goes to our reviewers, Eve Buzawa and Zoe Hilton, and the artists who designed our illustrations and appendices, Jennifer Spalding of Park Graphics and Thew Elliot. And, finally, our heartfelt thanks to the 36 experts from a wide range of disciplines who comprised the federal grant project's National Advisory Council. Their unlimited advice and invaluable recommendations are matched only by their unwavering commitment and dedication to improving services to crime victims.

CHAPTER 1

Community Response to Crime Victims

Introduction

> Everyone in our society has a right to life, liberty, and the pursuit of
> happiness, and the criminal justice system needs to find the means to
> ensure that these rights are honored and secured for the victims of
> crime.
>
> This will not be an easy task. It will require patience, goodwill, and
> experimentation. Some ideas will work while others will not. But the
> important thing to note . . . is that this experiment is already well
> underway. (Bird, 1984, p. viii)

Chief Justice Bird's remarks carry particular significance in this book because the
model the authors are advocating is part of the ongoing "experiment" necessary
to enhance the community's response to crime victims. It offers communities a
formula to explore themselves by using an eight-step model for creating community-specific protocol to enhance their response to crime and its victims. The model
is called the Protocol Development Cycle. The term *cycle* indicates that once the
eight steps are completed, they are repeated. The development of protocol is a
cyclical process, with the results of each completed cycle used during the next cycle
as the basis for making adjustments to the protocol. This is important because as
new developments become available—statutory changes, scientific advances for
evidence collection, information system technology, or simply additional services
available for referrals—they should be incorporated, or at least considered for
incorporation, into the protocol. Without continuous maintenance, a protocol
quickly becomes outdated or relegated to a shelf and no longer used.

Three years in the making, this model began in 1991 while the authors were
working for the National Victim Center on a federal grant project titled *Looking*

Back, Moving Forward: A Multidisciplinary Approach to Law Enforcement and Sexual Assault. (The project was later renamed *Looking Back, Moving Forward: A Program for Communities Responding to Sexual Assault.*)[1] The purpose of this project was to provide training and technical assistance to law enforcement officers, prosecutors, victim services, and medical professionals to promote sensitive treatment of sexual assault victims. This, in turn, would encourage victim participation in criminal proceedings, a motivation often lacking with victims of sexual crimes.

During the grant application phase, the request for proposal narrative suggested that a model multidisciplinary protocol addressing the needs of sexual assault victims be developed as part of the project. This model protocol was to become available to other communities for adaptation and adoption. As part of the *Looking Back, Moving Forward* project, a group of experts from varying disciplines were brought together to review existing protocol and discuss the elements necessary to create a "model" multidisciplinary sexual assault response protocol. At this meeting, one expert suggested that a "model protocol" would not necessarily be the best approach because each jurisdiction operates differently depending on its regulations, legislative mandates, available resources, and community culture. What seemed to be needed was a "how to" guide that would assist communities in defining and developing their own protocol. It was from this revelation that the authors began their "experimentation" on the eight-step Protocol Development Cycle. Before the authors began, however, background information was researched to answer such questions as the following:

1. How has the victims' role in criminal actions evolved and what has the impact been on crime victims?
2. Can the victims' role be expanded and their needs better met through a multidisciplinary community response system?
3. How can the system become more "victim centered" and use victim service professionals more effectively?

This chapter will explore the answers to these questions to provide the basis for the creation of the eight-step Protocol Development Cycle.

Evolution of the Victims' Role in Criminal Actions

Early in history, criminal law was essentially law for victims. Victims of crime exercised significant influence over the administration of justice, and they played a central role in the enforcement of society's rules. Most criminal sanctions involved redress to the victims, typically in the forms of compensation and restitution. This victim-centered attitude came from 11th-century Anglo-Saxon England, where the criminal law was a system of compensatory justice in which victims received monetary payment for offenses of various kinds:

The compensation for inflicting a wound one inch long under the hairline was 1 shilling; for cutting off an ear, 30 shillings; for cutting off a nose, 60 shillings; for knocking out a front tooth, 8 shillings; a back tooth, 4 shillings. . . . The payment for knocking out a man's eye was 66 shillings, 6 pence; if the eye remained in the head, only two thirds of that amount was due. The rape of a virgin required a compensation of 60 shillings; if she were [sic] not a virgin, only 16 shillings were [sic] due her . . . even homicide, if it were [sic] committed openly and not in secret, could be atoned for by a payment to the victim's kin, the amount corresponding . . . to the monetary value set on a person's life depending on the ranking in society. (Greenberg, 1984, p. 80)

Among the consequences of the Norman invasion of England, however, was the introduction of the concept that a crime against the king was ultimately a crime against the state. This had profound implications for the Anglo-American legal system (Bard, 1985, p. 43).

The current limitation of the role of the crime victim to that of a witness is also partly the result of the emergence of a system of public prosecution during the American colonial period. By the time of the American Revolution, all 13 colonies were under British political control. They were populated mostly by British colonists who brought with them the British common law tradition. During the 17th century, when the colonies were being settled, the British legal system was primarily a system of private prosecution. This system gave victims or their kin the right to bring and prosecute cases against criminal offenders. Yet, seeking private justice could be very burdensome to the victim in terms of time and money. It was during this time of settlement that public prosecution was developed and gradually superseded the private system (Gittler, 1984, pp. 124-125).

After the colonial period, the office of the public prosecutor continued to develop. One of the most significant changes that occurred was the switch from the appointed prosecutor to the elected one. According to Gittler (1984), "the impetus for this shift was the democratization of the American body politic, which began in the 1820s, was highlighted by the election of Andrew Jackson in 1828, and continued up to the civil war" (p. 131). Later, the characterization of the public prosecutor changed again by becoming a member of the executive, rather than the judicial, branch of government and the judicial and prosecutorial functions were clearly separated. These changes in the role and characterization of the public prosecutor served to consolidate prosecutorial power and discretion and elevate it to the level we see today.

Over the past few centuries, the defendant and the state evolved as the two parties with legal standing in criminal proceedings. The victim was virtually forgotten and became the "party without an institutionalized voice in the legal process" (Bard, 1985, p. 43). Accompanying these trends were some basic ideas, which Paul Hudson (1984, p. 24) characterizes as the "modern ideology of the criminal justice system."

1. A crime is primarily an offense against the government rather than a private wrong.
2. The government, because it acts for the good of the citizenry, cannot be held accountable for its mistakes or negligence in the administration of criminal justice.
3. Specially trained professional officers are better at controlling crime and seeing that justice is accomplished than the private citizens or victims of the offenses.
4. Victims are useful to the system as information sources and witnesses; their interests are not important to the system and could interfere with the efficient administration of justice.
5. Because of the great power of the state and the potential for abuse, persons accused or suspected of committing a crime need to be protected with an array of procedural rights and privileges.

Older ideas about the criminal justice system were replaced by this ideology of the criminal justice system. These older ideas included the notion that government has a duty to protect citizens from criminal acts, and that crime victims have the right to be made whole for their losses incurred by criminal activity. Over the past 30 years or so, American society has slowly awakened to the plight of the crime victim. The older ideas are being rekindled and the magnitude of crime victimization has forced people to confront the issue as a matter of public policy.

Many of the first efforts to revitalize the rights of victims focused on the development of crime victims' compensation programs. These initiatives originated in other countries. It was English magistrate Margery Fry who wrote in 1951, "we have seen that in primitive societies this idea of making up for wrong has wide currency. Let us once more look into the ways of earlier man, which may still hold some wisdom for us" (U.S. Department of Justice [DOJ], 1988, p. 2). In 1963, New Zealand started the first crime victims' compensation program and Great Britain followed suit in 1964. In the United States, federal crime victims' compensation legislation was first introduced in 1964 and the first state program was enacted in California in 1965.

In some ways, the 1964 Kitty Genovese case may have helped the long process of acknowledging the victim. Coming at the beginning of a spectacular rise in crime rates, this case was a much-publicized incident of a rape and murder occurring in plain view of a number of people who chose to ignore the victim's call for help. "As a media event, the public was presented with a shocking reality on one hand, and with a vivid symbol of society's unresponsiveness to victims on the other" (Bard, 1985, p. 45). That same year, Goldwater's conservative Republican campaign placed "crime in the streets" at center stage for the first time in presidential politics.

After his landslide election, Lyndon Johnson could not ignore the issue and appointed the President's Commission on Law Enforcement and the Administration of Justice. The Commission pioneered methods for assessing the nature and extent of criminal victimization in America and its recommendations resulted in the Law Enforcement Assistance Administration (LEAA) a decade later (Bard, 1993). Some of the studies were initiated to explain the reluctance of crime victims to become witnesses, and to uncover ways in which the criminal justice system could become more responsive to victims while improving the criminal justice process. Researchers and criminal justice system officials soon learned that public dissatisfaction was so great that nearly two thirds of all crimes went unreported. The LEAA was lodged with the responsibility of improving the criminal justice system's approach to crime victims and witnesses. Its program, the Citizens' Initiative Program, awarded three 1 million dollar grants resulting in the development of 19 new victim service programs, including eight prosecutor-based victim assistance programs. By 1979, more than 50 million dollars in LEAA funds were allocated for victim assistance programs. There is little question that available funding from the LEAA provided the initial impetus for the establishment of victim assistance programs within criminal justice agencies. The LEAA met its demise in 1980 due to a sunset clause that eliminated its funds (Bard, 1985, p. 45; DOJ, 1985, p. 6; DOJ, 1988, p. 3).

At the same time that prosecutor-based victim assistance programs were developing, grassroots victim advocacy groups were organizing with the purpose of obtaining equity through law. By the early 1970s, people began to speak of the "victims' movement," and the silence that surrounded rapes and domestic violence began to break. Victims started to realize that they were not responsible for the crimes committed against them. Strongly influenced by the women's movement and civil rights movement, rape crisis and domestic violence centers multiplied and by 1979 could be found in at least one community of every state.

There was also another important influence on the growth of the victims' movement, "the spillover of street crime from economically disadvantaged areas of our cities to affluent sections and the suburbs. For the first time in the modern era, citizens with political power were experiencing unaccustomed powerlessness as victims" (Bard, 1993). This new class of crime victims wanted more than acknowledgment of their plight; they wanted the right to participate in the criminal justice system. This prospect of victim participation met with resistance because it threatened the established patterns of justice. Studies showed that prosecutors, defense attorneys, and judges operated together as they shared the mutual goal of disposing of cases as quickly as justice would allow. To introduce the victim as the fourth party in decision making would slow down an already overburdened docket.

Research (Hernon & Forst, 1984), however, disproved this theory that victim participation would slow the wheels of justice. "Indeed, studies revealed that a sense of participation was more critical to victims' satisfaction with the criminal justice system than how severely the defendant was punished" (Kelly, 1990, p. 175). Increased levels of satisfaction, in turn, increased the likelihood that victims would cooperate with the criminal justice system.

Much of this revelation about victim participation was uncovered by the President's Task Force on Victims of Crime (DOJ, 1986, p. 1). On April 23, 1982, President Reagan established this task force to address the needs of millions of

Americans and their families who were victimized by crime each year (President's Task Force on Victims of Crime, 1982). This nine-member task force held public hearings in six cities across the country receiving testimony from nearly 200 witnesses (professionals, both in and out of the criminal justice system, as well as citizens who had been victimized by crime). Its Final Report, issued in December 1982, focused on three fundamental needs of victims:

1. Victims must be protected.
2. The justice system must be responsive to victims' needs.
3. Victims need assistance to overcome the burdens imposed by crime.

The task force presented a series of 68 recommendations addressed to the legislative and executive arms of government at the state and federal levels; components of the criminal justice system; the medical, legal, educational, mental health, and religious communities; and the private sector. These recommendations comprised a comprehensive set of proposals that articulated the scope and the needs of crime victims. Included in these recommendations was a call for federal legislation providing funding to assist state crime victims' compensation programs, as well as federal funding to be matched by local revenues to assist in the operation of government programs and private, nonprofit victim service agencies that make comprehensive assistance available to victims of crime.

In October 1982, the first major piece of federal victims' rights legislation was enacted, the Federal Victim and Witness Protection Act. Shortly thereafter, the Office of the Attorney General (1984) published guidelines for implementing the act's goal of providing fair treatment to crime victims in the federal criminal justice system. These guidelines incorporated "victim and witness concepts beyond those set forth in the Victim and Witness Protection Act, in particular, pertinent recommendations of the President's Task Force on Victims of Crime" (p. 2).

Over a decade later, victims' rights legislation has flourished and now exists in every state. The vast array of enacted legislation has expanded legal protection afforded to victims and mandated that criminal justice agencies become more responsive to those who have been harmed by crime (Young, 1992, p. 39). For example, victims must now *be notified of*

- court schedule changes in 42 states;
- final disposition of cases in 31 states;
- parole of offender in 47 states;
- pardon of offender in 16 states;
- work release of offender in 34 states;
- prison release of offender in 34 states; and
- escape of offender in 34 states.

Several states also require consultation with victims at various decision points during the criminal justice process. For example, 26 states require that victims be consulted during plea negotiations.[2] (A requirement that was upheld in *People v. Stringham* [1988], when a guilty plea was determined to have been properly vacated by the sentencing judge when he found that the victim's survivor had not been permitted to comment on the plea.)

A total of 45 states require or allow written victim impact statements at sentencing, with 24 states explicitly permitting a victim's statement of opinion about the sentence. In addition to those protections afforded to all crime victims, there are specific protections for victims of sexual assault in the 46 states that have enacted rape shield laws and the 50 states that enacted privacy protection laws (Young, 1992, p. 40). In general, these laws prohibit the disclosure of victims' identities. They also shield victims from disclosure of their counseling and prior medical records, as well as inquiries into their past sexual conduct.

Despite the passage of a vast array of victims' rights legislation, crime victims still are not uniformly guaranteed the right to attend court proceedings. The defendant's right to remain in the courtroom is guaranteed by the Sixth Amendment to the Constitution. A national movement was formally organized in 1987 as the Victim Constitutional Amendment Network (VCAN) because of the belief that the victim's attendance at trial was critical (Kelly, 1990, pp. 179-180). To date, state constitutional amendments that afford crime victims the full spectrum of rights to be informed, present, and heard at all stages of the criminal justice process have been enacted in almost one half of the states (Legislative Database, National Victim Center [NVC], 1995).

The key question is whether or not these statutes actually accomplish their goals of greater participation within the criminal justice system and enhance assistance for crime victims. Research, funded by the National Institute of Justice seeking to answer this question, is currently being conducted by the National Victim Center. Other studies, however, suggest that a coordinated effort of criminal justice and community service agencies does increase the likelihood that crime victims will exercise their rights for greater participation in criminal proceedings and receive the services they need and deserve (Cohn, 1982). Regardless, most victims' rights legislation requires response from a number of disciplines and criminal justice agencies to comply with statutory requirements. Thus, a multidisciplinary effort for responding to crime victims can help encourage compliance and ensure that the goals of these legislative efforts will be met.

Expansion of the Victims' Role Through Interdisciplinary Efforts

Multidisciplinary response teams began in the late 1950s and early 1960s to improve services to abused and neglected children and their families. In 1978, the National Center on Child Abuse and Neglect defined a multidisciplinary team as "a group of service providers, both professional and paraprofessional, from a variety of disciplines, working together in the provision of diagnostic, treatment, prevention, and consultation services" (Keeney & Hall, 1992, p. 5). As the field grew, this definition expanded to encompass the entire intervention process from the initial interview through adjudication and treatment. Now used in response to victims of a broad spectrum of violent crimes, these teams provide a method of coordinating all response agencies into a cohesive, well-defined, and cooperative process that not only results in more successful investigation and prosecution of cases, but also provides a more effective and less traumatic response to victims and their families. In fact, the multidisciplinary team is now often referred to as an "interdisciplinary" team. The rationale is that "multidisciplinary" refers to several disciplines working on a case under some implicit or explicit procedures that might mean as little as separate case reports held together by a single staple. Interdisciplinary teams, in contrast, work alongside each other and provide an integrated analysis (Alexander, 1993, pp. 95-96). These professionals work so closely that they often develop strong professional and interdisciplinary attachments (Goldstein & Griffin, 1993, p. 93).

The primary goals of the interdisciplinary team include elimination of duplicative efforts by professionals, protection of crime victims from further trauma, successful investigation and prosecution of offenders, and assurance of services that best meet the needs of the victims and their families. To achieve these goals, the team must be actively involved in reviewing specific cases together, from the time of the initial interview until the case is retired.

Traditionally, each agency or profession has had a different role in the investigation and intervention process when a person is victimized. Their efforts to fulfill these roles and achieve agency goals may, however, result in further harm to the victim they are trying to help. For example, overinterviewing a victim can lead to additional stress and traumatization, causing a second victimization and often resulting in diminished cooperation with the criminal justice system. By working as a team, the need for multiple interviews can be dramatically reduced and delays in investigations and the provision of appropriate services will diminish. As the members of a team build working relationships, communication between agencies becomes easier and coordination of services improves. These teams are not meant to replace any existing agency or profession; they are intended only to strengthen and build interagency and professional relationships that enhance the community's response to crime and its victims. Each team must incorporate the unique characteristics of the community it serves and work to weave the existing service delivery system together in such a way that effective case management will occur through a more efficient means of resource use (Keeney & Hall, 1992, p. 8).

The interdisciplinary team provides many benefits for crime victims. According to the National Network of Children's Advocacy Centers Advisory Board (1990), these benefits include the following:

- The trauma experienced by the crime victim is reduced.
- Victims are more likely to receive prompt and ongoing services that are tailored to their specific needs and those of their families.
- More offenders are held accountable for their crimes.

- Professionals gain a better understanding of and respect for each other's roles, responsibilities, and expertise.
- More decisions regarding the prosecution of the offender are made with input from the crime victim or professionals acting on the crime victim's behalf.
- Cases are more quickly disposed of and are less likely to "fall through the cracks" in the system.
- Communities are better able to identify the gaps in the system, thereby furnishing critical information necessary to advocate for more resources and additional services.

On the other hand, interdisciplinary teams are not without their drawbacks. One consideration is that they can be expensive. Working in a cooperative environment often requires more travel time to a central location to discuss issues as a group. Salaries of staff can be costly; however, the additional time up front may save valuable time in the long run if it results in a more efficient system. According to Krugman (1984), other drawbacks include

- the likelihood of conflict when many people with diverse backgrounds and philosophies are brought together around a single issue;
- interference with the smooth functioning of the team by individuals who are either independent or, at the other extreme, are not able to work independently and need constant support; and
- lack of direction or coordination, which can result in a deterioration of the team effort and waste valuable resources through endless, undirected meetings. (p. 764)

It is clear, however, that a smooth running interdisciplinary team benefits both the system and the victim. Each of the drawbacks discussed in this text can be resolved with knowledge, understanding, and effort. Techniques such as conflict resolution or conflict management can be used to ensure that conflicts become productive elements in the group process.

As with any work unit, selection of individuals for the team is critical. Carefully developed role descriptions for team members will provide guidance during the selection process, and they should encourage a preference for individuals who embrace the team approach. If an independent or needy individual is selected to join the team, support from other members may be necessary to encourage that individual to cooperate or, if necessary, resign.

The most critical element in controlling drawbacks, however, is coordination. It is essential to find one individual whose primary role is to coordinate all efforts of the team. This person should be responsible for the timely distribution of information, including dates and deadlines, and logistics of team meetings or other means of communication among team members. If the drawbacks of the interdisciplinary team approach are identified and acknowledged during the formation stages of the group, they are less likely to hinder the process down the road.

Creation of a "Victim-Centered" System

As indicated in this chapter, victims' rights legislation has challenged criminal justice professionals to rethink their conceptualization of the crime victim as "just a witness." These statutory requirements have also caused some criminal justice agencies to develop their own victim/witness assistance programs, because many agencies realize that it requires different skills to work as a victim advocate than those possessed by most police officers, investigators, and prosecutors. Still, even with the onslaught of interdisciplinary programs that support crime victims and improve victim treatment—programs such as child abuse or family violence treatment teams—little has been accomplished in redefining the role of the victim from that of a witness to that of an informed, active participant who influences decisions concerning his or her case. For this reason, most programs, including victim/witness assistance programs in criminal justice agencies, are still mainly characterized as "system-centered" in that they articulate their goals in terms of system performance measured by the number of arrests, indictments, convictions, and so on. Just as traditional concerns by criminal justice agencies about arrests and convictions are valid, so too are crime victims' concerns about involvement in decisions affecting how their victimization is dealt with in the criminal justice system. Criminal justice personnel and victims need to see concepts—such as arrest, convictions, and victim involvement—as mutually supportive. The crime victim has an interest in the assailant's arrest, conviction, and sentencing. The criminal justice system needs victim cooperation to build a tighter case and to convict an accused assailant (Patterson & Boles, 1992, chap. 1, pp. 6-9).

The ideal system has the following characteristics:

- The need for crime victims to assume control over their own lives is recognized and supported.
- Cases are vigorously investigated.
- Offenders are apprehended and aggressively prosecuted in a timely fashion.
- Crime victims are kept informed at each stage of the proceedings.
- Crime victims are given the opportunity to express a preference for what they would like to see happen.

By definition, the ideal system must be an interagency, multidisciplinary effort—multidisciplinary because the skills necessary for investigation are different from those needed for prosecution or victim advocacy; interagency because these disciplines are usually found in different agencies and, to have an effective system, these agencies must work together ("interdisciplinary teams").

Victim service professionals have the most critical roles in ensuring that the interagency system functions effectively; for example, they bridge the gaps between the various agencies and disciplines, provide services related to victim assistance and advocacy, monitor compliance with victims' rights legislation, and serve as liaison between crime victims and criminal justice agencies (Patterson & Boles, 1992, chap. 7, pp. 1-2). Unlike other team members who serve victims at certain decision points in the case (law enforcement officers, prosecutors, medical personnel, and so on), many victim service professionals serve and assist victims from "start to finish." Thus, they are in the unique position to interact with other team members at each case decision point, which, in turn, helps facilitate effective communication with the victim and reduce additional trauma for that individual.

Victim service programs offer a variety of services such as

- providing crisis intervention and response at crime scenes;
- helping prepare crime victims for court;
- maintaining constant communication with victims and their families regarding case status;
- encouraging and supporting crime victims as active participants in their case;
- advocating for victims' rights and services;
- communicating the views and opinions of crime victims to other agencies and organizations (court, prosecutors, police, other service providers, and so on);
- securing appropriate services for crime victims and their families;
- protecting and ensuring victims' privacy;
- helping to prevent additional trauma and injury to crime victims; and
- ensuring that the system responds to victims and their families in an appropriate and timely manner.

The challenge for some of the traditional agencies, such as law enforcement and prosecution, is to modify their approach and become more "victim-centered." The difference between the criminal justice system of the past and that of the future is the explicit goal of expanded victim participation in case decisions. Victim participation in decision making not only benefits the crime victim (Koss & Harvey, 1991, p. 133), but also helps the criminal justice system perform better (Heinz & Kerstetter, 1979, p. 349). For these reasons, the system of the future will be "victim-centered."

Chapter Summary

The main focus of this book is to explore an eight-step model, called the Protocol Development Cycle, for creating community-specific protocol to improve response to crime and its victims. To create an effective model for protocol development, the authors thought it significant to conduct background research and define pertinent concepts. The three major areas of research include (a) the evolution of the victims' role in criminal actions; (b) the expansion of the victims' role through multidisciplinary efforts; and (c) the creation of a "victim-centered" system.

It is clear from the history of the victims' role in criminal actions that the crime victim, although previously a central character in the enforcement of society's rules during the antiquated system of compensatory justice, is currently little more than a witness for the government. During the past few decades, which focused on victims' rights legislation, there developed a movement to bring crime victims back into a mainstream role within the criminal justice system. To do so, victims needed the support and cooperation of many disciplines from a variety of agencies to keep them informed of criminal proceedings, allow them to be present and heard at key points during the criminal justice process, and assist them with their recovery from the trauma of victimization. An interdisciplinary effort that combines the talents of multiple disciplines from several agencies has become the vehicle in many communities for improving treatment of crime victims.

Although victim treatment has vastly improved in recent years, most crime victim response systems involving criminal justice agencies are still "system-centered." To become "victim-centered" in its approach, the criminal justice system must have the explicit goal of expanded victim participation in case decisions and begin to measure success not only in terms of arrests, indictments, and convictions but also in terms of victim involvement.

One way to orchestrate the victim-centered orientation is through an interagency council, which is responsible for the development and implementation of protocol that enhances the community's and criminal justice system's response to crime and its victims. Chapter 2 discusses the interagency council, including its structure, membership, and goals.

Notes

1. A project of the National Victim Center in partnership with the American Prosecutors Research Institute and the Police Foundation. *Looking Back, Moving Forward: A Multidisciplinary Approach to Law Enforcement and Sexual Assault*, Cooperative Agreement No. 91-DD-CX-K038, funded by the Office for Victims of Crime and Bureau of Justice Assistance, Office of Justice Programs, U.S. Department of Justice. *Looking Back, Moving Forward: A Program for Communities Responding to Sexual Assault*, Cooperative Agreement No. 93-VF-GX-K003, funded by the Office for Victims of Crime, Office of Justice Programs, U.S. Department of Justice. Correspondence concerning these projects should be directed to the National Victim Center, Information and Library Services, 2111 Wilson Boulevard, Suite 300, Arlington, Virginia 22201.

2. Adapted from Young (1992). Funded by the Office for Victims of Crime, Office of Justice Programs, U.S. Department of Justice, Cooperative Agreement No. 91-DD-CX-K039. Statistics updated by the National Victim Center, Public Policy Division, from their *Legislative database* (1995).

References

Alexander, R. C. (1993). To team or not to team: Approaches to child abuse. *Journal of Child Sexual Abuse, 2*(2), 95-97.

Bard, M. (1985, Winter). Unblaming the victim. *Social Policy, 15,* 43-46.

Bard, M. (1993, October). *Keynote address.* Presented at the Federal Victim-Witness Coordinators' Conference, Baltimore, MD.

Bird, R. (1984). Letters of introduction. *Pepperdine Law Review, 11,* viii.

Cohn, A. H. (1982). Organization and administration to treat child abuse and neglect. In E. H. Newberger (Ed.), *Child abuse* (pp. 89-103). Boston, MA: Little, Brown.

Gittler, J. (1984). Expanding the role of the victim in a criminal action: An overview of issues and problems. *Pepperdine Law Review, 11,* 117-182.

Goldstein, J., & Griffin, E. (1993). The use of physician-social worker team in the evaluation of child sexual abuse. *Journal of Child Sexual Abuse, 2*(2), 85-93.

Greenberg, J. (1984). The victim in historical perspective: Some aspects of the English experience. *Journal of Social Issues, 40*(1), 77-101.

Heinz, A. M., & Kerstetter, W. A. (1979). Pretrial settlement conferences: Evaluation of a reform in plea bargaining. *Law & Society Review, 13*(2), 349-366.

Hernon, J., & Forst, B. (1984). *The criminal justice response to victim harm* (National Institute of Justice Publication). Washington, DC: U.S. Department of Justice.

Hudson, P. S. (1984). The crime victim and the criminal justice system: A time for change. *Pepperdine Law Review, 11,* 23-62.

Keeney, K. S., & Hall, K. K. (1992, September/October). Multidisciplinary teams improve services, maximize use of limited resources. *NRCCSA NEWS, 1*(3), 5, 8.

Kelly, D. P. (1990). Victim participation in the criminal justice system. In A. Lurigio, W. Skogan, & R. Davis (Eds.), *Victims of crime: Problems, policies, and programs* (pp. 172-187). Newbury Park, CA: Sage.

Koss, M. P., & Harvey, M. R. (1991). *The rape victim: Clinical and community interventions* (2nd ed.). Newbury Park, CA: Sage.

Krugman, R. D. (1984). The multidisciplinary treatment of abusive and neglectful families. *Pediatric Annals, 13,* 761-764.

Legislative database. (1995). Arlington, VA: National Victim Center, Public Policy Division [Producer and Distributor].

National Network of Children's Advocacy Centers Advisory Board. (1990). *Best practices: A guidebook to establishing a children's advocacy center program.* Huntsville, AL: National Children's Advocacy Center.

Office of the Attorney General. (1984). *Attorney General's guidelines for victim and witness assistance.* Washington, DC: U.S. Department of Justice.

Patterson, J. C., & Boles, A. B. (1992). *Looking back, moving forward: A guidebook for communities responding to sexual assault.* (Available from the National Victim Center, 2111 Wilson Boulevard, Suite 300, Arlington, VA 22201)

People v. Stringham, 206 Cal. App. 3rd. 184 (1988).

President's Task Force on Victims of Crime. (1982, December). *Final report* (Publication No. 82-24146). Washington, DC: Government Printing Office.

U.S. Department of Justice, Bureau of Justice Assistance. (1985, March). *Program brief: Victim assistance program.* Washington, DC: Author.

U.S. Department of Justice. (1986). *Four years later: A report on the President's Task Force on Victims of Crime.* Washington, DC: Government Printing Office.

U.S. Department of Justice. (1988). *Report to Congress.* Washington, DC: Author.

Young, M. A. (1992). State of the law in victim's rights. In *The road to victim justice: Mapping strategies for service* (pp. 37-43). (Training manual available from the National Organization for Victim Assistance [NOVA], 1757 Park Road, NW, Washington, DC 20010-2101)

CHAPTER 2

Establishing the Interagency Council

Introduction

The concept of crime as a community concern serves as a starting point for transforming the criminal justice system's response to crime victims. In the context of community responsibility for addressing the issues of violent crime, the set of respondents may be enlarged beyond the traditional criminal justice system. By extending the responsibility for improving this response to the community, criminal justice agencies expand the resources they may mobilize to assist crime victims.

A victim-centered system begins with a core of criminal justice agencies, health care facilities, and victim service organizations, with appropriate linkages to other service providers in the community. Because each community is unique in its matrix of services, the composition of the *interagency council* will reflect the uniqueness of the community (Patterson & Boles, 1992, chap. 3, p. 9).

The community interagency council is an interdisciplinary, multiagency, victim-centered group responsible for developing and implementing protocol that improves the community's response to crime and its victims. Some of the responsibilities of its members include

- assessing the community's needs as they relate to violent crime;
- developing consensus concerning each agency's respective role in responding to the identified needs;
- formulating protocol reflecting the consensus;
- negotiating interagency agreements and formulating the cooperative relationships and responsibilities embodied in the written protocol;

- conducting training and technical assistance for agencies' personnel who have contact with or are responsible for services to violent crime victims; and
- monitoring, evaluating, and adjusting the protocol that govern the interactions of the interagency council with crime victims.

The primary goal for developing a victim-centered system by a community interagency council is to empower the crime victim to make choices. Other goals in a victim-centered response system that the interagency council can help achieve include the following.

- *Maintain the flow of information to victims concerning the status of their cases.*

As previously cited, one of the primary dissatisfactions that crime victims have concerning the traditional handling of their cases is the lack of information about the status of their case.

- *Make the views of victims known to the court on key decisions.*

Bail decisions, continuances, plea negotiations, dismissals, sentencing, and restitution are critical points at which victims want to have their opinions heard.

- *Identify and remove inconveniences for crime victims' participation in case handling.*

Crime victims should be permitted to be "on-call" for hearings, interviews, and trials while continuing their daily lives as normally as possible to minimize their financial and emotional hardships.

- *Preserve the privacy of crime victims.*

The names and addresses of crime victims—especially sexual assault, domestic violence, and child victims—should not be made public. Most states have enacted laws prohibiting public disclosure and publication of certain crime victims' identities. Many of these state laws also permit closed courtrooms at the discretion of the trial judge. Some states allow certain crime victims to use a pseudonym at all stages of the investigation and trial.

Criminal justice agencies also benefit from the interagency council's efforts to create a victim-centered response system. The following list contains some of these benefits:

- *Increase the cooperation of crime victims during the investigation, prosecution, and disposition of their cases.*

Informed crime victims who are given the opportunity to participate in case decision making are more willing to endure the ordeals of the criminal justice system.

- *Increase the reporting of crimes.*

A long-term benefit of a victim-centered community response system is a change in the perception of crime victims concerning how they may be treated. Those victims who are unwilling to participate due to concerns about public disclosure, further traumatization, and inability to achieve justice will, over time, learn that the system can be "victim friendly."

- *Increase political support for criminal justice agencies.*

As community perception of the criminal justice system changes from one in which only the criminal receives justice to one in which all parties, including the victim, receive justice, public acceptance of increased expenditures for criminal justice agencies will very likely result (Patterson & Boles, 1992, chap. 3, pp. 3-4). America Speaks Out: Citizens' Attitudes Toward Violence and Victimization, a national opinion poll conducted by the National Victim Center, found that 70% of the respondents would "probably or definitely" pay higher taxes to improve services to crime victims (National Victim Center [NVC], 1991, p. 7).

This chapter discusses what needs to be considered as communities address the creation of victim-centered interdisciplinary responses to crime and its victims, including the following:

1. *Membership of the Community Interagency Council.* Which agencies in the community are responsible for criminal cases and helping victims of violent crimes?

2. *Forming Advisory Committees.* What groups of individuals would offer valuable information for victim-centered protocol and support the activities of the interagency council?

3. *Tailoring Interagency Council and Advisory Committees' Membership to Meet Community Needs.* In addition to agencies with identified responsibilities, what other kinds of organizations or individuals should be part of, or offer consultation to, the interagency council?

4. *Networking and Forming Linkages to Meet the Needs of Distinct Crime Victim Populations.* What services are available from organizations specializing in providing assistance to identified populations? How can the interagency council access these services for eligible crime victims?

Interagency Council Membership

Membership of the interagency council should be viewed on two levels:

1. Agency Membership. The first level relates to the identification of the agencies that should be members of the interagency council for development of the protocol.
2. Individual Representatives. The second level pertains to the kind of representative each agency will have (agency director, division supervisor, line worker, or a combination of levels).

PARTICIPATING AGENCIES

For a community to have an effective interagency council, there are several agencies that must participate. These include the following:

Law Enforcement. The police department and other law enforcement investigative agencies in the jurisdiction served.

Prosecution. The state's attorney, district attorney, or other prosecution offices responsible for criminal cases.

Medical. Hospitals, emergency care centers, and other medical facilities responsible for treating victims of violent crimes, collecting forensic evidence during examinations of sexual assault or child abuse victims, or performing autopsies in homicide cases.

Victim Services. Nonprofit, community-based organizations, such as rape crisis or domestic violence centers, and system-based victim assistance programs, such as those operating out of police or prosecutor's offices.

These four categories of agencies are essential participants for formulating any communitywide response to violent crime because they are the key agencies that respond to crime and its victims, aiding them from the point of the victimization throughout the criminal justice process and, in some cases, beyond (Patterson & Boles, 1992, chap. 3, pp. 4-5). In most communities, however, other organizations and agencies should be considered for membership on the interagency council. These organizations should be selected on the basis of the nature of specific crime-related problems within each jurisdiction and on services available that might be used to improve response to crime victims. Some additional organizations that communities might want to consider include the following:

Social Services. Child protective service agencies are required participants when developing protocol for child abuse and child sexual abuse cases. In these cases, Child Protective Services (CPS) divisions of social service agencies are legally responsible for receiving and investigating reports of child abuse. Similarly, crimes against elderly victims—including abuses committed by family members, caregivers, and strangers—are often reported first to Adult Protective Services (APS) divisions.

In addition to CPS and APS responsibilities, social service agencies may provide homemaker services, food stamps, health care, and other services to income-eligible recipients. Crime victims may lose income or jobs, or be incapacitated, thereby becoming eligible for social services and public assistance. Other victims who receive public assistance at the time of the crime may need additional support because of their victimization. Social service agency participation on the interagency council can help clarify roles in investigating certain cases and build important interdisciplinary relationships, as well as expedite delivery of required services to victims of violent crimes.

Mental Health. Access to various types of counseling services, to cope with the psychological trauma and aftermath of violent crime, is an important component of comprehensive services for many crime victims. There are four primary approaches to mental health services for victims (Koss & Harvey, 1991, p. 156) and each may be offered by different agencies. These four approaches include

1. a single-session trauma debriefing procedure for recent victims;
2. individual reintegrative treatment for victims who seek therapy months or even years after their victimization;
3. group treatment with other victims; and
4. public education designed to reach victims who never sought formal services.

Community-based or system-based victim assistance programs can often fulfill the initial crisis counseling needs of the crime victims. Additional mental health resources, such as rape crisis or domestic violence centers, or police and prosecutor victim assistance programs, are required when necessary services are not available through organizations. Because more extensive services such as long-term therapy may be required for some victims, it is advantageous for victim services and mental health agencies to work together, sharing their respective expertise and resources to ensure that victims are provided with appropriate mental health care. Such teamwork can be facilitated under the aegis of the interagency council.

Courts. The judiciary occupies a unique position in the criminal justice system. Judges are charged with maintaining an impartial position between prosecution and defense. Direct judicial involvement with the interagency council may be viewed in some jurisdictions as a violation of the neutral position. On the other hand, some judges are beginning to realize that impartiality requires recognition that the victim has rights, too. Several judges have taken a lead role in bringing improvements for crime victims within the criminal justice system. These judges often seek opportunities for greater involvement in addressing the concerns of victims.

It may also be possible to have court participation through a staff member, absent the direct involvement of judges. Many courts have administrators who can represent the court on an interagency council. Court administrators often have extensive influence on judicial scheduling and facility considerations, two areas of potential victim impact. Another approach for court involvement is through citizen watch-dog groups. One such group, the Council for Court Excellence in Washington, DC, has undertaken studies of court operations at the request of the court. In communities where such groups exist, they may provide a valuable bridge between the court and the interagency council.

Members of the interagency council should review existing court rules pertaining to victim involvement in judicial proceedings and suggest revisions in those areas where victims are not afforded access, process, and privacy.

Such suggestions would reinforce the community's concern for sensitive treatment of crime victims by the court. Adaptation and understanding of court rules may also indicate areas where protocol will help build the interagency relationships necessary to ensure that victims are afforded their rights by the courts.

Probation, Parole, and Community Corrections. The involvement of community corrections with the interagency council is essential to ensure that crime victims' rights are protected after a conviction. Probation and parole agencies are responsible for supervising offenders while they are in the community by monitoring their activities and securing compliance to conditions for remaining in the community. The roles of probation and parole officials are critical to helping crime victims retain a sense of security when their assailants have community placements.

Probation officers work in concert with the prosecutor, defense attorney, and judiciary to make recommendations about the convicted offender's sentence. Such recommendations include, but are not limited to the following:

1. length of sentence;
2. restitution to help victims recover costs associated with the crime, including long- and short-term mental health counseling;
3. protective or stay-away orders to ensure the victims' security;
4. community service;
5. participation in treatment programs (particularly sex offender treatment programs); and
6. participation in education programs (such as programs that offer offenders insights about the impact their crimes have on themselves, their families, their communities, and their victims).

A victim's input into a convicted offender's sentence and relevant conditions is usually included in a presentence investigation (PSI) report, which is completed by the probation officer. In some jurisdictions, a written Victim Impact Statement (VIS) is attached to the PSI; in other communities, the probation officer interviews the victim to obtain input about sentencing and recommended conditions of probation.

Similarly, parole agencies possess authority that can have tremendous impact—both positive and negative—on the crime victim. In most cases (except in states with determinate sentencing), the sentenced term of imprisonment is much longer than the term an offender actually serves (U.S. Department of Justice [DOJ], 1991, p. 12). Therefore, parole hearings come as an unpleasant surprise to many victims. Crime victims need to be informed of and accorded any extended rights relevant to parole notification and input at parole hearings. The ideal situation would include support of a victim advocate at the hearing. Because most parole hearings are held in penal institutions, victim attendance and participation can be an intimidating and frightening experience.

When persons convicted of a crime are released into the community on either probation or parole, it is imperative that the victims are informed about their assailants' status. The interagency council should have representation from these agencies to help develop protocol directing that crime victims be provided with the name and contact information (24 hours per day) of the offender's probation or parole officer to receive status updates or information relevant to the offender's condition(s) of release. Community corrections representatives on the interagency council can also work with other council members and their agencies' administrators to help plan and develop victim sensitivity training programs for their personnel. Because most probation and parole staff positions are "offender oriented," such training programs will help these staff members to also view victims as clients and make their agency's overall mission more victim centered.

Correctional Institutions. In most communities, the correctional institution(s) will not be included as a formal member of the interagency council. There are linkages, however, that need to be made with these institutions concerning the physical location of the perpetrator and decisions to permit work release or furloughs. The interagency council must be knowledgeable about the types of corrections-based services that are available for crime victims and how these victims can access them. These services may include transfer, work release or furlough notification, information about offender education and treatment programs, and direct services or referrals for correctional personnel who have been victimized on- or off-the-job.

Schools/Colleges/Universities. Interagency councils should consider a wide variety of educational institutions as potential members. Many school systems, colleges, and universities have their own security forces, some with regular policing powers. Students may report crimes taking place on campuses to campus police, school administrators, or a trusted teacher. Experience has shown that schools are often reluctant to file official reports on some crimes, for example, sexual assault or domestic violence, due to possible negative publicity. In cases in which the assault was perpetrated by another student, it may be preferred to handle the case through internal discipline processes that give the perpetrator the "benefit of the doubt." Representation from these institutions helps reinforce that they are part of the larger community and establishes protocol that defines victim-centered, community responses to campus crimes.

The involvement of schools, colleges, and universities should also include input from professionals who have authority over educational policies, including school boards for primary and secondary schools, Boards of Regents for colleges and universities, and Boards of Directors for private institutions. Similarly, other education-related groups concerned about potential crimes on their campuses—including the Parent-Teacher Association, teachers' unions, and local professional associations of education employees—should be aware of interagency council activities and, when possible, provided the opportunity for input.

There are benefits to inviting educational institutions to become members of interagency councils; however, developing protocol that includes the reporting, investigating, and prosecuting of crimes that occur on campuses is not incumbent on the appointment of education representatives to the council. These benefits include closer coordination and communication, thereby enabling a more accurate assessment of violence on campuses, and creating easier access for support services to campus crime victims (Patterson & Boles, 1992, chap. 3, pp. 4-5).

Crime Victims' Compensation Agencies. All states and the District of Columbia have established victims' compensation programs (Young, 1992, p. 41). These programs generally provide payment to crime victims for injuries or loss of wages suffered as a result of the crime. To be eligible for this form of compensation, victims must report their crime to the police and cooperate with the criminal justice agencies. Each state also has specific eligibility requirements. In addition, the Victims of Crimes Act (VOCA) requires states to expand their benefits to include payment for mental health counseling, and to extend eligibility to include nonresidents and victims of federal crimes that occur within the state's borders.

Interagency councils should not assume that the existence of a crime victims' compensation agency means that victims in their community are aware of their right to compensation. A representative from the state crime victims' compensation agency should be considered for membership on the interagency council to ensure that protocol is developed that includes compensation information, referrals, and services for victims. At the very least, a representative should be invited to inform the interagency council about the state's crime victims' compensation program and about the processes involved in securing compensation for crime victims. The protocol should also define and delineate linkages with the compensation program's administrative agency. Such linkages can help prevent what have been characterized as "administrative delays" in making compensation payments to eligible victims (Young, 1992, p. 42).

LEVEL OF REPRESENTATION

Each level of personnel in agencies participating in the interagency council will play an important role in the development and implementation of the protocol. These roles will be explored further in the chapters that explain each of the eight steps of the Protocol Development Cycle. At this point it is sufficient to say that each agency's key representative on the interagency council should be an individual who thoroughly understands the roles and responsibilities of all agency personnel and how critical tasks within the agency are accomplished. This individual should also have a considerable measure of decision-making authority on how his or her agency is represented in the protocol. Agencies should avoid selecting representatives who serve purely as a conduit of information on interagency council activities to the decision makers of the organization. This type of representation severely hinders the progress of protocol development and implementation.

Most agencies select division chiefs or directors as their key representative. These individuals have

1. appropriate decision-making authority to contribute effectively to the protocol development process;
2. access to the chief executive to keep him or her informed of and updated on critical council activities, as well as the ability to influence the timely review and official sign-off of the final protocol document; and
3. access to other personnel within the agency and authority to assign them writing responsibilities for sections of the protocol or other critical tasks that need to be performed.

Advisory Committees

The interagency council consists of representatives from agencies or organizations that have a role specified in the protocol. Individuals will generally not have a responsibility identified in the protocol; therefore, interagency councils should consider establishing one or more *advisory committees*. The purpose of the advisory committee is to receive input from representatives of organizations, as well as individuals, that are not members of the interagency council but have an interest in its activities.

The interagency council can benefit from the establishment of advisory committees for several reasons. Advisory committees

- provide counsel and support on issues pertaining to the interagency council's overall mission and specific objectives;
- provide knowledgeable experts and input for protocol development and implementation from both individuals and special interest groups; and
- can review and make suggestions relevant to specific sections of the interagency council's protocol in which the advisory committee has expertise.

A variety of populations should be considered for interagency council advisory committees, including but not limited to crime victims, the media, elected officials, and religious leaders. These examples are discussed next.

CRIME VICTIMS' ADVISORY COMMITTEE

Interagency councils should strongly consider establishing a crime victims' advisory committee. This committee allows for critical input from crime victims to ensure that protocol is victim-centered. This group can review protocol and advise the interagency council about its impact on crime victims' needs. Its members are in the unique position of providing first-hand, personal experiences that can help "fine-tune" the protocol.

Victims selected for the advisory committee should meet specific qualifications formulated by the interagency council. Individuals who have recently been victimized or are currently involved in the investigation and prosecutory stages of the criminal justice system should not be considered.

Victim advocacy organizations may be good sources for nominations of individuals who are sufficiently recovered from their victimization so that serving on the advisory committee would benefit both themselves and the interagency council (Patterson & Boles, 1992, chap. 3, pp. 6-7).

MEDIA ADVISORY COMMITTEE

Media involvement is critical to the ultimate success of the interagency council. Media participation, however, does not involve direct services to crime victims, but, rather, helps inform the community about the interagency council and educates the public about efforts to treat victims more empathetically in the criminal justice system.

The *media advisory committee* should participate in the development and review of protocol that addresses privacy issues and the confidentiality of crime victims' identities (unless the victim provides permission to be identified). Training sessions for media representatives, conducted by members of the interagency council, can help reporters understand that freedom of the press is not compromised by protecting the identity of a victim. Experience has shown that the media can be "pro-victim" when reporters, editors, and other media representatives are given guidelines and assured that the facts they need to fulfill their roles will be available. Conversely, inviting media advisory committee members to provide training to interagency council personnel can provide a foundation of understanding for media concerns.

A media advisory committee can also help interagency council members understand *how the news media works*. A basic understanding of news media relations—including how media operations are structured, how deadlines are met, and how types of information are deemed "newsworthy"—can help the interagency council achieve maximum public relations and community outreach impact with limited time and resources.

ELECTED OFFICIALS' ADVISORY COMMITTEE

There are many elected officials who play significant roles in developing and implementing public policies that affect crime victims and those who serve them. Federal, state, and local officials make important decisions relevant to program funding, development, and implementation. They also have significant concerns about any activities, programs, and services that might improve the jurisdictions they were elected to serve and, in particular, their specific constituents.

An advisory committee of elected officials can keep the interagency council informed about how its protocol and related programs affect the "bigger picture" of the community it serves. Information about community awareness efforts, funding available for crime victims' services, and public policy affecting victims and the agencies that serve them can be provided to the interagency council by the *elected officials' advisory committee*. Conversely, the interagency council can educate this advisory committee's members about crime victims' needs and the necessity for public policy reforms.

CLERGY ADVISORY COMMITTEE

Members of the clergy and their congregations are often key players in the crime victim's emotional and spiritual recovery. Through the efforts of national organizations such as the Spiritual Dimension of Victim Services and Neighbors Who Care, representatives of America's religious community are receiving training and technical assistance to help them better meet the needs of victims of crime. An advisory committee comprised of representatives from the religious community can help clarify the important roles that members of the clergy have in aiding crime victims, and it can recommend ways in which religious congregations can support the efforts of the interagency council (Patterson & Boles, 1992, chap. 9, pp. 11-13).

Tailoring Interagency Council and Advisory Committee Membership to Meet Community Needs

The word *community* has a variety of possible meanings. It may refer to a geographic location or it may refer to an identifiable population of individuals living within a geographic area. For example, within the community of Albuquerque, New Mexico, there is a *university community*. There are other types of communities based on religious beliefs, sexual orientation, ethnicity, or economic status. This listing is not complete but it illustrates that, in addition to geographic boundaries, communities may be defined by shared cultural, religious, and economic ties.

Membership in a community helps give individuals an identity in the context of shared characteristics, such as belief systems, values, economic status, or perceived suppression by the "mainstream" majority. Most people belong to multiple communities that are identified by geographic, economic, cultural, and religious boundaries. Such affiliations can strongly influence crime victims' reactions to their victimization. To the extent that the victim sees the community as supportive, compassionate, and accepting, membership in that community may be therapeutic. To the extent that the victim sees that community as judgmental, hostile, and skeptical, that community is toxic to the crime victim (Koss & Harvey, 1991, p. 115).

Normally, interdisciplinary/multiagency planning to respond to crime and its victims within a community defines the jurisdiction as a geographical region. An important part of the planning process is the realization that most jurisdictions are not homogeneous in their make-up; therefore, consideration must be given to the *communities within the community*. Some of this diversity is discussed in the sections on urban and rural communities; closed communities; federal properties; and communities with significant cultural, religious, or ethnic groups. This chapter also considers the roles that these groups might play in the development of victim-centered protocol.

URBAN COMMUNITIES

Responding to the challenges of crime within urban jurisdictions falls under the "good news—bad news" scenario. The "good news" is that there are usually more resources that may be brought to bear on the problems; the "bad news" is that there are almost always more problems than the resources available to address them. One planning issue is more efficient use of existing resources to create a victim-centered system.

Certainly the magnitude of the crime problem in urban areas and the bureaucracies created to address crime result in a more complicated system. The system is more complicated not only for the criminal justice personnel assigned to criminal cases; it is also more complicated for the victims of crime. The urban system may have a tendency to deliver "assembly line justice," with individual victim identities replaced by case numbers. The planning challenge is to develop a system so that crime victims are insulated from underlying complexities.

Another way of looking at this issue is to consider that, for those working within the criminal justice system, one criminal case is just another of perhaps hundreds or even thousands of cases. For the victims, it may represent the single, most traumatic event in their lives. Criminal justice personnel must be able to investigate, prosecute, and adjudicate the mass of criminal cases while giving all victims a sense that their individual cases are important.

The interagency council can increase the level of service to individual crime victims by involving these victims in the decisions affecting their cases. Another way the interagency council can improve services to these victims is through coordinating efforts and assigning specific responsibilities for keeping victims informed of case progress (Patterson & Boles, 1992, chap. 3, pp. 8-9).

RURAL COMMUNITIES

Rural jurisdictions are characterized by large geographic, sparsely populated areas in which certain communities serve as hubs for agriculture and commerce. Populations are generally smaller and often the systems developed to address crime are less formal than their urban counterparts. Rural areas present their own unique challenges to both the criminal justice system and crime victims. The Rural Task Force of the National Coalition Against Domestic Violence (NCADV; 1991) notes that:

> There are many commonalities for those of us who identify as rural women. We face lack of resources, isolation, small town politics, few funding resources, little transportation, fewer telephones, and problems keeping shelters or safe home locations confidential. (p. 7)

As in cases of domestic violence, both availability and accessibility of specialized services for all victims of violence are likely to be issues in rural areas. Services, when they are available, are likely to be located in the hub communities, while victims may be several hours away. As the Pennsylvania Coalition Against Domestic Violence points out in their *Rural Outreach Manual:*

> Because there is no public transportation, women without vehicles cannot . . . keep counseling appointments. Poor roads often prevent women who do have cars or trucks from driving long distances. . . . Some women never leave the communities in which they live, and they

may not know of any other place to go. (NCADV, 1991, Appendix A, p. 5)[1]

The availability of medical personnel to treat crime victims or gather forensic evidence in such crimes as sexual assault or child abuse, may create special problems in rural areas that are notoriously underserved in the health care fields. The gathering of evidence is important; however, the lack of available medical care for crime victims is of greater importance. The interagency council can address these problems by creating regional resources and providing transportation to crime victims in need of medical services.

On the positive side, natural helping systems have evolved in many rural communities. Identification of these resources is an important facet when planning a rural response to crime and its victims. Churches have played a central role in addressing the social service and mental health needs of rural residents, and they serve as a good source for volunteers and needed funds (NCADV, 1991, p. 53). In rural jurisdictions, clergy representation may be essential for an effective inter-agency council.

CLOSED COMMUNITIES

Closed communities are those to which public access is limited. Often these communities have established their own internal mechanisms for dealing with crime. American Indian reservations, school campuses, and military bases are examples of closed communities. Interagency councils serving jurisdictions encompassing closed communities should examine the dynamics of crimes involving members of closed communities. Some dynamics are discussed next.

American Indian reservations. American Indian reservations not only present a specific set of cultural perspectives on issues related to violent crimes, especially domestic and sexual crimes, but also represent unique jurisdictional concerns related to

- the location of the crime (on or off the reservation);
- the victim's identity (Indian or non-Indian);
- the perpetrator's identity (Indian or non-Indian); and
- the jurisdiction of the tribal law enforcement and judicial branches.

The resolution of these concerns results in tribal, Bureau of Indian Affairs (BIA), Federal Bureau of Investigation (FBI), or state jurisdiction for investigation of the crime and determines whether it will be prosecuted in tribal, federal, or state court.

Although these appear to be *systems* issues, they also have an impact on victims. For example, when a crime victim is an American Indian and the crime was committed in a non-Indian jurisdiction bordering a reservation, the surrounding community may not feel responsible for addressing the victim's needs. There may be an expectation that the tribe should assist the victim. The tribe, however, may believe that because the crime took place off of the reservation, victim intervention and services should be provided by the jurisdiction in which the crime occurred. Consequently, the victim could easily "fall through the cracks." The interagency council's planning process should address basic issues about the nature of the crime problem in the entire community—on and off the reservation—including the following:

- Who are the victims?
- Who are the perpetrators?
- What services are available to American Indian crime victims off of the reservation?
- What services are available on the reservation?
- How are linkages achieved between reservation-based services and non-Indian criminal justice agencies?

When American Indian victims who live on reservations are assaulted in non-Indian communities, maintaining communication with victims may present unique challenges. Telephone communications have improved considerably on most reservations; however, many reservations are in remote areas and some have no direct telephone access. This presents two problems. First, it may be hard to notify victims what the status of their case is or that their presence is required. A second difficulty is that of minimizing inconveniences and expenses associated with case-related appearances that occur because of the distances that victims may need to travel. Addressing the first problem requires that the interagency council establish a liaison with law enforcement agencies on reservations for the purpose of relaying communications to victims. Addressing the second problem requires (a) planning for appearances; (b) avoiding continuances; and (c) providing transportation, meals, and lodging.

In jurisdictions with sizable American Indian populations, or in close proximity to reservations, the interagency council should consider membership of reservation law enforcement, tribal court, victim service personnel, or all of these to help with the planning and protocol development processes, and should establish linkages between the Indian and non-Indian communities. An advisory committee composed of American Indians is also appropriate to help address the needs of that population (Patterson & Boles, 1992, chap. 3, pp. 9-12).

School Campuses. Another example of a closed community is a school campus. School campuses were addressed previously in this chapter when discussing interagency council membership. Issues specific to the closed community of college campuses will be addressed here.

As stated earlier, colleges may be reluctant to report crimes for fear of negative publicity. They may select to handle offenses through internal disciplinary structures that favor the offender. Or, in cases of specific crimes, they may not recognize that the crime occurred. This is most typical in the case of sexual assaults because these assaults are frequently perpetrated on campuses by acquaintances of the victims.

Campus violence, particularly sexual assault, has received national attention over the past decade. The issue of campus rapes is one that affects both the university and the local community and, therefore, is one that both communities must address through cooperation between local law enforcement agencies and campus security services.

The Campus Sexual Assault Victims' Bill of Rights Act of 1991[2] provides for increased protection to victims of sexual assaults on campuses. The *Crime Victims Digest* (Ramstad, 1991, pp. 1-2) published a summary of these rights, which include the right to

- have sexual assaults investigated by criminal and civil authorities;
- be free of pressure from campus authorities to refrain from reporting crimes, or to report crimes as lesser offenses;
- have the same representation as the accused at any campus disciplinary proceeding, and to be notified of the outcome;
- have full and prompt cooperation and assistance in obtaining the evidence necessary for proof of criminal sexual assault, including a medical exam;
- be made fully aware of and assisted in exercising state or federal legal rights to test sexual assault suspects for communicable diseases;
- have access to existing campus mental health and victim support services;
- be provided housing that guarantees no unwanted contact with alleged sexual assault assailants; and
- be allowed to live in campus housing free of sexually intimidating circumstances with the option to move out should such circumstances be present.

Once again, the need for communication, cooperation, and joint planning in the development of a victim-centered approach are essential ingredients in effectively addressing this problem and other campus crimes; thus, campus representation on the interagency council should strongly be considered. A student advisory committee may also be helpful in identifying the needs of this population.

Interagency councils should not overlook crimes that take place in elementary and secondary schools—public, private, and church operated. Protocol also needs to address the reporting and investigating of offenses and provide assistance to the young victims of crime. When addressing crimes against children, the interagency council should coordinate its protocol with Child Protective Services.

Military Bases. Military bases present a unique set of conditions that may involve both problems and opportunities. Most military bases contain a variety of services that are available to members of the military and their dependents who are crime victims, including medical care and counseling. Some victims may not feel comfortable using these services, possibly due to concerns about privacy and confidentiality. For example, an officer's wife who is the victim of spousal assault will have no choice but to have the offense reported if she seeks treatment at a military facility. Within the armed services, the only guarantee of confidentiality is with the chaplains.

Military bases also create demands on the civilian system with large populations of young, single males seeking social outlets in adjacent civilian communities. Restricted public access to military bases may hamper the community's investigations of criminal cases involving military personnel. When military officials have disciplined the offenders, victims may not have had the opportunity to be heard, or may not even know that an action was taken to redress the crime.

Increased attention is being given by the Department of Defense and all branches of the military regarding criminal behavior by military personnel. Adverse publicity caused by the sexual assaults of female officers at a 1992 meeting of the Tailhook Association, as well as incidents of sexual harassment at some of the military academies, has led to mandated training for military commanders, law enforcement personnel, and social service professionals. The priority of the military to improve their response to crimes perpetrated against female personnel may provide an excellent opportunity for closer relationships between military base officials and the interagency council. These officials should be involved in the planning and development of any protocol that links this closed community with the surrounding civilian community for the purpose of responding to military crime victims.

FEDERAL PROPERTIES

Federal properties include federal buildings, national parks and monuments, and national forests. Some of the planning considerations pertaining to these federal jurisdictions are similar to American Indian reservations, but there are significant differences. Victims of crimes in national parks, at monuments, or in national forests may be transient vacationers whose residences are thousands of miles away from the crime scenes. For those responsible for the investigations, prosecutions, and adjudications of these crimes, the long distances become management issues and may determine whether a case is even pursued. For crime victims, these distances may mean that no referrals are made for victim intervention and support services. Consequently, victims may not receive the services needed to help them with the emotional distress caused by the crime.

In planning the community response to crime and its victims, representatives from federal properties should be consulted and given the opportunity to participate in the development of protocol. Designating an appropriate interagency council member to ensure that transient victims receive referrals for services in their home communities is an important protocol element for jurisdictions with federal properties.

COMMUNITIES WITH SIGNIFICANT CULTURAL, RELIGIOUS, OR ETHNIC GROUPS

Up to this section of the chapter, the primary focus of the community "definition" has been the geographic boundaries, even in closed communities with specific ethnicities such as American Indian reservations. There are other kinds of communities, however, that are tied together by cultural, religious, or ethnic commonalities. These commonalities may also have less formal geographic boundaries; for example, individuals with similar cultural, ethnic, or religious backgrounds may constitute neighborhood communities. Some of these neighborhoods function as centers for cultural activities and may offer services for individuals living outside of the neighborhood but who identify with the cultural, religious, or ethnic make-up of the neighborhood.

Urban communities tend to be more diverse in their composition than rural communities. Consequently, they will have more identifiable communities within the community. Nonetheless, the possibility of identifiable cultural and ethnic groups in rural areas, for example, the Amish in Pennsylvania, should not be overlooked. These groups not only have distinct needs but often have resources in their communities to meet these needs, such as special crime victim support programs or interpreter services for victims not proficient in the English language.

The planning process for community response to crime and its victims should include participation of representatives from organizations serving the population that is identified as a community within the community. The nature of the participation may include providing testimony at hearings called to gather information about public perceptions of the community's needs as related to crime victim response. It may also be as an official member of the interagency council or on an advisory committee addressing the needs and services specific to that victim population.

The criteria used to select representation and the kind of participation in such groups should include

- the magnitude of crimes affecting the population (including an estimate of unreported crimes);
- public perceptions of the criminal justice system's response to crimes against the population;
- the need for specialized victim services for victims from the identified population; and
- the availability of victim services targeted at the specific population.

The eight-step model described in future chapters of this book will provide specific directions for conducting a Community Needs Assessment, which will help the interagency council identify ethnic, religious, and cultural groups; the needs, issues, and concerns each one brings to the victim-centered approach; and the community resources that are available to address the needs of these groups. The following sections provide an overview of pertinent information related to diverse population groups and crime victim responses (Patterson & Boles, 1992, chap. 3, pp. 13-16).

Crime Victims of Diverse Ethnic Backgrounds. Many different cultures and ethnic groups are represented in communities across the country. Persons from any ethnic background—African Americans, Asians, Hispanics, American Indians, Pacific Islanders, and other ethnic groups—may become victims of crimes. Interagency councils need to be aware of the different ethnic groups and cultures in their communities and address their needs and concerns in the protocol.

Identifying every distinct cultural and ethnic group, as well as the diverse needs and issues each represents, is impossible in this book. The issues and considerations described on the following pages serve as some examples of the types of specific needs presented by different cultural and ethnic groups.

- *Consider the negative impact and stigma associated with some crimes.*

In some cultures, the stigma attached to certain crimes such as sexual assault may be overwhelming, particularly for women. As a result, crime victims may not report or discuss the crime. In the Asian community, for example, the fear of being ostracized or shamed as a result of a sexual assault is so great that women often do not report the crime. If the crime is reported, women may feel so ashamed that they may either turn to prostitution or kill themselves as a result (Chicago Police Department, 1990).

- *Consider the victim's inability to discuss some crimes with a person of the opposite gender.*

Again, sexual crimes affect this particular concern. As stated earlier, in some cultures women are too ashamed or fearful to speak about sexual assault. This fear can be exaggerated by the actions of the criminal justice system when it is insensitive to the needs of such victims. For example, Hispanic women often find that speaking to men about sexual assault is particularly uncomfortable.

- *Consider differing cultural governments.*

Still some cultures have their own "community" or "government" to address problems. For example, American Indian communities have their own sets of norms, rules, and regulations, and are governed by their own laws (as discussed in the Closed Communities section of this chapter).

Representatives from agencies serving specific ethnic or cultural groups can be valuable members of the interagency council in developing a victim-centered system responsive to the cultural needs and norms of a multicultural society. What is acceptable in certain cultures may not be acceptable in others. Behaviors such as making eye contact with victims, using certain words or terms, and pointing fingers at someone or something need to be considered in developing protocol to deal with various population groups.

The interagency council may need to "do things differently" when working with crime victims from different cultural and ethnic backgrounds. For example, victims from other countries may have little knowledge of the American criminal justice system and may need the process explained in greater detail, language barriers may necessitate the use of interpreters, and interviewers of a certain age or gender may be necessary to help crime victims feel more comfortable.

Another issue may be the crime victim's immigration status. Because victims may illegally reside in this country or be fearful of being returned to their own country, the likelihood of their reporting a crime is diminished. Illegal aliens may believe that they will be deported as a result of calling attention to themselves. The interagency council protocol should include procedures for confronting immigration and victimization concerns so that all parties involved provide these victims with accurate information and respond to them in a victim-centered manner as well as according to accepted procedures.

Religious Support for Crime Victims. Many crime victims indicate that their victimization was made bearable due to their religious beliefs or because their spiritual leaders provided counseling and emotional support. As previously mentioned, churches and religion have had a tradition of being the sources of emotional as well as spiritual support, especially in rural communities.

In some urban areas, neighborhoods reflect the influences of dominant religions and their values and beliefs. In these areas, crime victims may be affected both positively and negatively. If the religious community provides support and understanding, they may be positively affected. Crime victims may be negatively affected if the religious community is judgmental and blames victims, especially in cases of sexual assault and domestic violence.

There are several ways in which religious communities can participate in the interagency council's activities and assist crime victims. Churches have meeting rooms that may be available for peer support and other kinds of counseling sessions as well as for interagency council meetings. Churches may also be involved in such support services as clothing collections to ensure that sexual assault or other victims have replacement clothes to wear home from the hospital after their clothing is taken for forensic examination; lock replacement for victims whose homes or businesses have been broken into; transportation to help victims attend court and medical or mental health appointments; and many other voluntary activities that support victims of crime.

Members of the clergy can also be important participants in counseling crime victims. In many communities, the only kind of counseling may be through a local pastor, priest, or rabbi. Many police departments have members of the clergy, who serve as chaplains, on call. On military bases, clergy are the only source of confidential counseling and consultation for crime victims. The interagency council's protocol should provide guidelines for contacting a crime victim's religious leader after first obtaining authorization from the victim. The interagency council should provide training for clergy to maximize their abilities to assist victims of violent crimes (Patterson & Boles, 1992, chap. 3, pp. 16-18).

Gay and Lesbian Crime Victims. Cultural differences are not always based on religious, ethnic, or racial origins. Gays and lesbians represent a distinctly different culture and are estimated to be up to 10% of the population. Gay and lesbian victims may be reluctant to report crimes, especially sexual crimes, because they assume they will be met with insensitive comments or unfair treatment from criminal justice personnel. In addition, many gay and lesbian victims whose sexual orientation has been previously unrevealed, may be concerned that the crime will generate publicity that will "out"[3] them. In cases such as sexual crimes, domestic violence, and stalking or hate crimes, repeated victimization may occur when victims fear being "outed" and do not report crimes. They may fear that disclosure of their sexual orientation will jeopardize their jobs, housing, or custody of their children (Chicago Police Department, 1990). These fears have been exacerbated in some jurisdictions, such as in Oregon and Colorado, by recent attempts to remove antidiscrimination protection.

Gay and lesbian crime victims may not volunteer information about their sexual orientation and criminal justice personnel should not assume a victim's sexual orientation based on physical characteristics. Most gays and lesbians do not match the stereotypical portrayals of effeminate men and masculine women.

Like other religious, cultural, or ethnic groups, gays and lesbians are prime targets for hate-motivated crimes. These crimes tend to be physically and mentally brutal and violent. Assaults that are motivated by bias and hatred are often accompanied by derogatory name calling, graffiti, or both.

Relationship crimes also exist and must be acknowledged within this population. Just as with heterosexual couples, gays and lesbians may force or attempt to force their partners to submit to sexual activity, or may be involved in violent relationships. In addition, other sexual crimes such as acquaintance rapes occur within this population when gays and lesbians are sexually assaulted by another gay or lesbian they know or with whom they are involved as part of a social relationship. Criminal justice personnel and victim service agencies must consider any nonconsensual sex as a crime, *irrespective of the sexual orientation of the victim or the perpetrator.* When characteristics of crime victims become more important than the crime committed against them, the victim is being blamed for who he or she is and, therefore, is made more vulnerable to further victimization.

In developing and planning for protocol to address the needs of gay and lesbian crime victims, the interagency council should identify and provide access to services for these victims in an unbiased, supportive manner. In larger cities, appropriate referral agencies may be located in gay and lesbian communities and could be valuable members of the interagency council, or an advisory committee may be advantageous to help identify and address the needs of this population of crime victims. Some criminal justice agencies have appointed liaison officers to gay and lesbian communities to improve the delivery of services (Patterson & Boles, 1992, chap. 3, pp. 18-19).

Distinct Populations of Crime Victims

The previous section discusses diversity within the community by focusing on communities within communities, which have either geographic boundaries or a geographic locus such as a neighborhood that functions as a "magnet" for individuals sharing particular commonalities. In this section, other dimensions of diversities are discussed, those commonly found throughout the community.

The following discussions describe the needs of several distinct population groups as they relate to the development of a victim-centered system addressing crime and its victims. Distinctions are made on the basis of the age of the victim, disabilities, homelessness, and relationship to the primary crime victim. Each of these conditions may require specific protocol to accommodate the needs of the affected crime victim. The categories introduced are not all-inclusive. The discussion of distinct population groups can be used to guide community planning for developing and implementing victim-centered approaches for other population groups as well. It is important to note that whenever a suggestion is made that other individuals—family members, friends, advocates, or caregivers—may help communicate with, or otherwise provide support to crime victims, their involvement should occur only after victims have given their consent.

AGE-BASED DISTINCTIONS

There are two groups of crime victims who have needs based on their ages: children and the elderly. The distinctive needs of children are somewhat recognized by statute; elderly crime victims must, for the most part, rely on administrative provisions for attending to their specific needs (Patterson & Boles, 1992, chap. 3, p. 20).

Crime Victims Who Are Children. Over the past decade, there has been widespread formation of multidisciplinary teams to address child abuse in the community. In fact, most multidisciplinary protocol in this country that exists for communities was developed to address crimes against children. Interagency councils should collaborate with any existing multidisciplinary child abuse teams to ensure that all segments of the community population are served and that efforts are not duplicated. In some communities, the child abuse multidisciplinary team and the interagency council will consist of many of the same agencies and have considerable overlap in personnel. In communities where there are no child abuse multidisciplinary teams, the interagency council's protocol should include child abuse victims, and a representative from Child Protective Services (CPS) should definitely be a member of the council.

Child victims pose many challenges for victim-centered systems, the primary one being the child victim's limited involvement in making case-related decisions (virtually impossible for young children, but extremely important for older children and adolescents). It is possible, however, for a parent, *guardian ad litem,*[4] or court-appointed special advocate[5] to represent the interests of young children and participate in case-related decisions. Child victims may be too young or too fearful to report the crime, or they may be confused about the "assault" because the perpetrator was in a trusted or caretaker role. In developing and planning for a victim-centered system, interagency councils must also consider legal procedures that differ in child abuse cases.

Many attempts to help child victims, particularly those of sexual assault, result in unintended consequences:

> Survivors may be ill prepared for the response to the disclosure. They may feel blamed or manipulated. The type of help they want may not be the intervention that is offered, as when a sexually abused child wants her father to stop molesting her and the intervention takes her away from the home—a move she did not want. (Roberts, 1990, p. 211)

When addressing the needs of child victims, the interagency council should conduct a comprehensive inventory of services and resources responsive to the varied needs of children. The inventory should include CPS, school systems, youth-serving agencies, medical facilities, and nonprofit organizations.

In recent years, communities have made substantial advancements in developing and using a team approach to address child abuse. Evaluations of such programs indicate the most effective methods for the team to use in child abuse cases. Interagency councils should rely on research results and the experience of these teams when developing their protocol.

Crime Victims Who Are Elderly. Elderly victims present particular issues and challenges for the community interagency council. One of the factors complicating the planning and provision of services for this population is that many elderly victims are isolated and either cannot or do not report the crimes committed against them. In communities with large elderly populations—those with nursing homes and senior centers, or those with neighborhoods that attract elderly citizens—the specific needs of the elderly should be addressed in the protocol and Adult Protective Services (APS) invited to participate on the interagency council. A senior citizens' advisory committee may also be appropriate in some jurisdictions to ensure that the needs of this population are met.

Elderly victims are one of the most vulnerable populations. These victims may be severely traumatized, feel ashamed or embarrassed about their vulnerability or assault, and are often uncomfortable discussing the crime with family members or friends, if they are able to discuss it at all. In the case of sexual assault of an elderly victim, this crime is often accompanied by other crimes, such as robbery. When reporting other crimes, these elderly victims may choose to ignore or conceal the sexual assault.

Many elderly persons have difficulty making their own needs known to others. Some have always seen themselves in the role of caretaker, such as the parenting role, and it is difficult to express the need for assistance. Others have physical disabilities or impairments, such as hearing loss, which may exacerbate their problems or limit their communication abilities, while intensifying their need for services.

Interagency council members need to recognize that elderly crime victims may require a variety of different types of services and resources, some of which may not specifically relate to the crime. Helping elderly victims deal with their emotional and physical well-being, as well as the issues related to their victimization, is an important consideration. Close teamwork between victim service providers and social service agencies may facilitate the delivery of needed services.

Many communities have programs specifically for elderly victims. For example, Court Watch in Milwaukee, Wisconsin, provides information, support, and assistance to older victims and witnesses in court (Roberts, 1990, p. 82). In developing protocol to address the needs of elderly victims, the interagency council should consider the necessity of

- conducting an immediate assessment of each elderly victim's needs and responding as quickly as possible;

- providing information, assistance, and referrals;

- providing support throughout the processes (accompanying victims to physical examinations, court-related interviews, court, and so on);

- identifying and reaching out to other local community groups for support services to elderly victims (churches, AARP chapters, Meals on Wheels, and so on);

- maintaining communication and working relationships with local organizations (police, senior centers, associations of professionals that work with the elderly, and so on);

- handling various emergency situations (stalking of elderly victims, health-related problems that were caused by the crime or affect the criminal justice process, and so on);

- modifying the courtroom to facilitate access by elderly victims (wider aisles for wheelchairs, witness stand at floor level, earphones providing amplification of the proceedings, and so on);

- providing emotional support and guidance (crisis counseling, peer survivor network, victim advocate, and so on);

- ensuring confidentiality (including the victim's family members and friends unless consent is given by the victim); and

- being flexible in providing specific assistance needed by elderly victims (offering services or conducting interviews within the home, arranging transportation, providing 24-hour support, and so on). (Patterson & Boles, 1992, chap. 3, p. 23)

CRIME VICTIMS WITH DISABILITIES

The Americans With Disabilities Act of 1990, Public Law 101-336, requires criminal justice personnel to enable full participation by individuals with disabilities, including those who are hearing impaired or deaf, visually impaired or blind, physically disabled, or developmentally disabled. Specifically, the Americans With Disabilities Act (1990) requires "public entities" (defined as "any state or local government, department, agency, specific purpose district, or other instrument of a state or local government") to change "rules, policies, or practices" and provide "auxiliary aids and services" to remove "architectural, communication, or transportation barriers." The following sections describe some of the adjustments in the criminal justice policies and practices that provide crime victims with disabilities the fullest possible access to the criminal justice system and victim services. Representation of individuals with disabilities on an advisory committee or, if employed by a member agency, on the interagency council may be advantageous when developing protocol that affect these populations.

Hearing-Impaired or Deaf Crime Victims. Individuals who are hearing impaired (those who have some ability to hear) or deaf (those who cannot hear at all) have specific methods of communicating. According to the National Association of the Deaf (1984, p. 84):

> People with normal hearing usually communicate by talking and listening. Often, they pay attention only to the words that are spoken and the tone of voice used to say them. Moreover, most people also use facial expressions and gestures to emphasize their words. Faces, hands, and arms can be very useful tools when communicating with others.
>
> People who are hearing impaired may, with hearing aids, hear some of what is said, but it may not sound much like what a person with normal hearing would hear. Because of this, it is important to make spoken messages as visible as possible. Usually a combination of methods works well.
>
> Remember that hearing-impaired people vary widely in the ways in which they communicate and the skill with which they do it. However, most hearing-impaired people communicate by using
>
> - sign language;
> - facial expressions and gestures;
> - speech-reading;
> - mime (acting out the idea);
> - listening;
> - speech;
> - drawings;
> - writing; and
> - a combination of any or all of these.

All criminal justice and victim service agencies need to ensure that their personnel are trained to work with hearing-impaired and deaf crime victims or have immediate access to trained referral sources for assistance. Such personnel need, at a minimum, to understand the different aids for communications on which individuals who are hearing impaired and deaf often rely: hearing aids, lipreading, sign language, and writing.

Hearing aids: When taking statements from or interviewing a crime victim who is hearing impaired and wears a hearing aid, the interviewer should articulate and pronounce each word clearly. If an individual who wears a hearing aid has difficulty responding to or participating in a conversation with criminal justice or victim service personnel, it is possible that the hearing aid is not functioning, possibly from damage during an assault or other crime. Victim service professionals should help find services that will adjust, repair, or replace hearing aids that were damaged during the commission of a crime. Some state Crime Victims' Compensation programs will pay for this.

Lipreading: Many individuals who are hearing impaired or deaf rely on lipreading to understand what others are saying. When interviewing crime victims who are lipreaders, the interviewer should face the victim and speak clearly, but without exaggerating normal lip movement. Even when addressing other individuals present, the speaker should try to face the person who is lipreading.

Sign language: A common sign language is American Sign Language—a manual-visual language communicated through the hands and face, in which signwords develop and evolve through natural processes based on sign communicators' needs, culture, and manual-visual communication needs (National Association of the Deaf, 1984, p. 84). Other sign language systems include finger spelling and manual English. Like spoken languages, sign languages include locally specific idiomatic expressions of which the interpreter needs to be aware.

Writing: The interviewer may write down the questions or statements for a crime victim who is hearing impaired or deaf, and that victim may respond orally or in writing. If the victim responds in writing, both questions and responses should be preserved as evidence.

Persons responding to crime reports should not make assumptions about how hearing-impaired victims communicate. These victims should be asked (or written a note asking) how they would like to communicate. A question can be phrased: Would you be more comfortable using American Sign Language and having an interpreter? It may also be necessary for investigators to use nontraditional communication methods to collect information and help the crime victim feel more comfortable. For example, in the case of sexual assault, the use of anatomical dolls may help victims identify the nature, details, and circumstances of the assault (Goddard, 1989, p. 2). In addition, the interagency council protocol should address the possibility of videotaping these interviews, as there might not be a written transcript.

Persons responding to crime reports of individuals who are deaf may assume that it is all right to ask family members to interpret for the victims; however, this is not an appropriate role. Family members may have also been traumatized by the crime and, in some instances, a family member may even be the perpetrator. More important, this assumption does not take into account the victim's needs. Victims may feel particularly vulnerable after a crime and find it extremely uncomfortable having family members present during the interview. Whenever possible, victims should be consulted about family members serving as interpreters and give their consent.

The interagency council must also address the issue of telephonic communication with hearing-impaired and deaf crime victims. Telecommunication devices for the deaf (TDD) display words and enable communication with deaf and hearing impaired-individuals. Although some telephone companies offer a *relay* service whereby an individual with a TDD equipped telephone can have messages relayed by an operator to an individual without a TDD, the confidentiality of the crime victim and the information relayed might be compromised through such a system. To comply with the Americans With Disabilities Act, every criminal justice agency should have at least one telephone equipped with TDD and personnel trained to use it. Some victim service agencies may also be equipped with a TDD (Patterson & Boles, 1992, chap. 3, pp. 24-26).

Visually Impaired or Blind Crime Victims. As with crime victims who are hearing impaired or deaf, victims who are visually impaired or blind present some unique considerations for the interagency council. The term *visually impaired* indicates that there is limited sight; the term *blind* is a legal term indicating severe loss of sight. The planning process and community assessment can help the interagency council identify access to local resources for victims who are visually impaired or blind. During the interview process, as well as subsequent steps of the case investigation and court processing, victims can also identify the resources and support systems that they need.

The interagency council should not make assumptions about a victim's inability to provide details about the crime. For example, crime victims who are visually impaired may not be able to identify their assailants by sight; they may, however, be able to identify the assailants' voices or other characteristics (an Illinois sexual assault victim was able to identify her assailant by his body odors). With the help of support services, victims may be able to provide extensive information about the crime.

Some specific accommodations that the interagency council can provide for visually impaired or blind crime victims include the following:

Validating victims' abilities to use other senses for making identification of assailants. Expert witnesses can testify about how individuals who are blind or visually impaired may be able to compensate for their loss of vision by increasing their reliance on other senses.

Accommodating victims with assistance devices. Some visually impaired or blind individuals have canes or guide dogs that enable them to be more mobile and self-sufficient than would otherwise be possible. A blind or visually impaired crime victim must have complete control over these assistance devices at all times. Guide dogs should be permitted in the courtrooms with the victims (Baldarian & Waxman, 1985).

Providing documents with large type for visually impaired crime victims. Most word-processing programs allow for scalable fonts. Documents intended to be read by visually impaired victims should be printed in larger type to facilitate reading. (This is also useful for elderly crime victims whose eyesight may be diminished.)

Providing documents printed in braille for crime victims who are blind and know how to read braille. Braille is a system of writing consisting of raised dots on a special paper that are read with the fingertips. The interagency council should consider preparing general information in braille for crime victims who are blind (Patterson & Boles, 1992, chap. 3, pp. 26-27).

Physically Disabled Crime Victims. Individuals with physical disabilities are those who may use wheelchairs, braces, crutches, canes, or a combination of these to facilitate or assist their movements. Full participation in the criminal justice system may mean that special accommodations are necessary to transport these crime victims to court and other case-related proceedings. It may also be necessary for the court to install ramps or make other building alterations to provide complete access for physically disabled persons and to comply with the Americans With Disabilities Act.

In addition to the more apparent access issues, physically or sexually assaulted victims may have distinct emotional needs. Their lack of mobility may increase their sense of vulnerability to further assaults. In some cases, the perpetrator may be a caretaker the victim trusted to provide essential care (Chicago Police Department, 1990). In these circumstances, crime victims with physical disabilities may have difficulties trusting anyone to assist with their care.

Developmentally Disabled Crime Victims. Another distinct population whose needs must be considered in the interagency council protocol is the developmentally disabled. The term *developmentally disabled* encompasses a broad variation in degrees of disability and includes "mental retardation, cerebral palsy, or other conditions that interfere with normal development and cause difficulties in communication, thinking, and mobility" (Baldarian, 1992, p. 8).

A primary issue in responding to crime victims who are developmentally disabled is determining their levels of comprehension and communication. Criminal justice and victim service personnel should not assume that a developmentally disabled person is an incompetent witness. The same qualifiers used to determine if a child is a competent witness may be used to determine if a developmentally disabled person—even if the disability is severe—is competent to testify.

Developmentally disabled victims may be unable to think in the abstract, may not understand terminology used during the interview process, or may answer questions in a way they believe interviewers would want them to answer. The key to meeting the needs of this population is found in the mental maturity—not chronological age—of the victim.

Developmentally disabled persons may be prime targets for crime because of their vulnerability. For this reason, reports should be handled seriously and procedures developed to accommodate the particular needs of these crime victims, including

- interviewing the reporting witness(es) first (if other than the crime victim) to determine the probable level of functioning of the victim, and then interviewing the victim;
- interviewing the victim in comfortable surroundings—at home or another familiar place away from the crime scene, if possible;
- being patient and making necessary accommodations to address the victim's needs;
- making the victim feel safe (no longer in danger);
- using developmentally appropriate, simple, nonleading questions during the interview process;
- letting the victim use familiar phrases and terminology (or slang) to explain the crime;
- being compassionate and concerned; and
- asking for assistance and support from caregivers—after they have been ruled out as suspects and, whenever possible, with the permission of the victim—during and following interviews. (Chicago Police Department, 1990)

HOMELESS CRIME VICTIMS

Homeless persons present some difficult challenges to communities, not only because of their economic status and needs, but because they are frequent and vulnerable targets of crime and assault. Because most homeless victims are unable to give law enforcement or other support agencies telephone numbers or addresses for follow-up assistance, there is a low probability that cases will be prosecuted. In an informal survey conducted by the Chicago Police Department, more than 88% of their homeless population claimed they were victims of assault. Few reported the assault to the police.

In developing a victim-centered approach for working with homeless crime victims, creativity and perseverance are key. Treating homeless crime victims with dignity and respect is, however, equally important. There are several other ways communities can become more sensitive to the needs of homeless crime victims and be more victim-centered in their approach:

- Victims can be given specific times, places, and telephone numbers to call to discuss further details of the case, obtain support services, or obtain assistance.
- If victims are staying in a shelter, assistance can be sought from shelter administrators (with victims' consent) to allow them to make or receive calls related to the crime.
- Third parties can be identified by victims to serve as information links (a friend, clerk at a transient hotel, or relative).
- Homeless crime victims can be encouraged to come into the police department or other agencies whenever assistance is needed.
- Specific locations (soup kitchens, shelter facilities) can be used to meet with victims. (Chicago Police Department, 1990)

SECONDARY CRIME VICTIMS

The trauma and devastation of violent crime are not experienced solely by those directly victimized (or the *primary victims*). They extend to many others known as *secondary victims.* They may be spouses or partners who need to find ways to deal with the crime committed against their loved one. They may be parents who feel tremendous guilt because they did not protect their child from being victimized. They may be friends or even coworkers who are trying to help the victim cope with the aftermath of the crime.

In developing protocol for a victim-centered system, the interagency council should recognize the needs and concerns of secondary victims and consider resources to meet their needs. Such resources and services may include support groups, crisis counseling, homemaker or child care services, and long-term psychological counseling (Patterson & Boles, 1992, chap. 3, p. 31).

Chapter Summary

The interagency council consists of organizations or agencies with major responsibilities for responding to crime and the expressed commitment to implementing victim-centered protocol. These include law enforcement agencies, prosecutors' offices, victim service organizations, and medical facilities. Although these are the four critical organizations or agencies necessary on every interagency council, each council must also be configured to meet the unique needs of its community. The eight-step protocol development cycle includes an Inventory of Existing Services that helps interagency councils identify additional organizations for membership. These organizations may include social service agencies, schools, colleges or universities, mental health facilities, courts, probation departments, correctional institutions, Crime Victims' Compensation programs, or other criminal justice and human service agencies.

In addition, interagency councils should create advisory committees comprised of individuals who are not affiliated with agencies that have primary responsibilities for responding to crime, but who can offer information and consultation to ensure that the protocol is victim-centered and complies with any statutory requirements. Advisory committees may include crime victims, clergy, the media, or public policymakers. Each community should identify which groups of individuals would best assist their interagency council by serving in an advisory capacity.

As part of the process of planning and implementing a victim-centered system, community interagency councils should ensure that they

- conduct a thorough assessment and identify population groups that require specialized victim assistance services;
- identify and access appropriate and necessary community resources and services to meet the needs of these distinct populations; and
- develop protocol that is sensitive to unique concerns and needs, and is flexible and adaptable to individual differences.

The interagency council must address the issues and concerns of distinct population groups for its protocol to reflect a victim-centered approach. The underlying premises and principles for dealing with any distinct population are that attention should be focused on the needs of the individual victim, that training criminal justice personnel to identify and respond to the needs of specific victim populations is a crucial component in providing comprehensive services, and that stereotypes and personal or professional biases have no part or role in a victim-centered system. Interagency council and advisory committee membership should reflect these philosophies and be used to help ensure that victims of distinct populations do not "fall through the cracks" within the criminal justice system and while seeking assistance to help them with the aftermath of crime.

Notes

1. Because the citation comes from a report addressing the needs of domestic violence victims, in which females are more prevalent than male victims, the pronouns *she* and *her* are used. This is intended only to imply that rural conditions for all violent crime victims may be similar, not that all victims would be female.

2. The Campus Sexual Assault Victims' Bill of Rights Act of 1991 was enacted as an amendment to the Crime Awareness and Campus Security Act of 1990 (20 U.S.C. § 1092) in March 1992.

3. "Out" as used here describes the revelation that a person is gay or lesbian. It refers to the expression "out of the closet." Within the gay and lesbian community, the decision to reveal one's sexual orientation is very personal.

4. *Guardian ad litem* is a term referring to a representative, usually an attorney, appointed by the court to represent the interests of the child.

5. Court-appointed special advocates (CASAs) are volunteers, trained to represent the interests of the child in court proceedings. Usually CASAs are not attorneys.

References

Americans With Disabilities Act of 1990, Pub. L. No. 101-336, § 2, 104 Stat. 328 (1991).

Baldarian, N. J. (1992). RAPPORT model aids victims with developmental disabilities. *NRCCSA News, 1*(4), 8.

Baldarian, N. J., & Waxman, B. J. (1985). *Rape treatment recommendations for disabled people.* (Available from the National Criminal Reference Service at 1-800-732-3277, Referenced Accession No. 113494)

Campus Crime Awareness and Campus Security Act, 20 U.S.C. § 1092 (1990).

Chicago Police Department. (1990). *Detective division protocol for sex crimes investigations.* Unpublished manuscript, Chicago Police Department, Chicago, IL.

Goddard, M. A. (1989). *Sexual assault: A hospital/community protocol for forensic and medical examination.* (Available from the National Criminal Justice Reference Service, P. O. Box 6000, Rockville, MD 20849-6000, Reference No. NCJ 123273)

Koss, M. P., & Harvey, M. R. (1991). *The rape victim: Clinical and community interventions* (2nd ed.). Newbury Park, CA: Sage.

National Association of the Deaf. (1984). *Basic sign communication: Student materials.* (Available from the National Association of the Deaf, 814 Thayer Avenue, Silver Spring, MD 20910)

National Coalition Against Domestic Violence, Rural Task Force. (1991). *Rural resource packet* (2nd ed.). (Available from the National Coalition Against Domestic Violence, P. O. Box 34103, Washington, DC 20043)

National Victim Center. (1991). *America speaks out: Citizens' attitudes toward violence and victimization.* (Available from the National Victim Center, 2111 Wilson Boulevard, Suite 300, Arlington, VA 22201)

Patterson, J. C., & Boles, A. B. (1992). *Looking back, moving forward: A guidebook for communities responding to sexual assault.* (Available from the National Victim Center, 2111 Wilson Boulevard, Suite 300, Arlington, VA 22201)

Ramstad, J. (1991). Campus Sexual Assault Victims Bill of Rights Act of 1991. *Crime Victim's Digest, 8*(5), 1-2.

Roberts, A. R. (1990). *Helping crime victims: Research, policy, and practice.* Newbury Park, CA: Sage.

U.S. Department of Justice. (1991). *Violent crime in the United States* (Publication No. NCJ-127855). Washington, DC: Author.

Young, M. A. (1992). State of the law in victim's rights. *The road to victim justice: Mapping strategies for service* (pp. 37-43). (Available from the National Organization for Victim Assistance [NOVA], 1757 Park Road, NW, Washington, DC 20010-2101)

CHAPTER 3

Protocol Development Cycle Overview

Introduction

Interagency councils, by definition, consist of representatives from a variety of disciplines, each with its own terminology. Because the same words do not always have the same meaning for all of the disciplines represented on interagency councils, definitions must be established by each council for use in its jurisdiction.

One example of this is *protocol,* a term that is more familiar to clinical than to legal disciplines. Because it is not a term common to all disciplines, and because it is central to the function of the interagency council, the concept of protocol must be thoroughly understood by all members of the interagency council before they embark on the protocol development process.

This chapter defines what we mean when we use the word *protocol* and offers an overview of the eight-step protocol development process for use by the interagency council.

Protocol

To assist in the development of the federal grant project guidebook (*Looking Back, Moving Forward: A Guidebook for Communities Responding to Sexual Assault*) from which this text is derived, the authors conducted a national search to obtain copies of relevant protocol. Medical personnel, law enforcement officers, prosecutors, and victim service professionals from across the country were alerted to this extensive resource collection effort. The purpose of this search was to obtain the broadest collection of existing protocol relating to the sensitive treatment of sexual assault victims.

Over 200 documents were received in response to the search. Although the criteria for submission were specific, the materials varied in their scope and nature—from a 500-page detailed description of the procedures for handling sexual assault cases to a 2-page agency brochure. The diversity of the materials received indicates that the respondents had different perceptions, and some confusion, about what the term *protocol* means.

OPERATIONAL DEFINITION

For the purpose of developing interdisciplinary, multiagency guidelines for assisting crime victims, the authors define *protocol* as: "The product of negotiations in which agreements are made and documented to create guidelines, and assign roles and responsibilities for community interagency council participants in responding to victims of crime" (Patterson & Boles, 1992, chap. 2, p. 8).

As we break down this definition into constituent parts, the elements of protocol are

> *product:* a tangible outcome;
> *negotiation:* a process of issue resolution between participating agencies;
> *agreement:* consensus shared among team members;
> *documentation:* in written form;
> *guidelines:* rules for agencies' involvement in cases and in response to crime victims; and
> *roles:* functions for agencies within the parameters established by guidelines.

PRODUCT

The concept of protocol as a product is important. Product connotes effort invested in its creation. Effective protocol requires effort by those who develop them. The nature of the interdisciplinary/multiagency protocol for crime victims is such that, even if standard protocol were available, it would need to be customized for each venue to accommodate the unique characteristics of different jurisdictions. There is no "off-the-shelf" protocol for universal application. Many jurisdictions, however, have developed protocol for specific disciplines or have some type of protocol in place for case management. Reviewing any existing protocol (whether it is called protocol, policies and procedures, or standard operating procedures) is always a good starting point for interagency councils. This protocol establishes existing procedures and provides the baseline for change.

NEGOTIATION AND AGREEMENT

Some of the responsibilities for addressing crime in the community are indisputable, such as those established by statute. Relevant statutes should be reviewed, discussed, and clarified by interagency councils to ensure that communities are in compliance, and that all parties understand their appropriate roles.

Negotiation will be required in those areas where the responsibilities are less clear and in which new interagency relationships are being established, for example, developing guidelines to address information sharing between victim service professionals and prosecutors or law enforcement investigators. The idea of sharing information with noncriminal justice agencies may be unconventional for some law enforcement agencies; however, if victim service professionals are to assist investigators by acting as a conduit for information between law enforcement and crime victims, information sharing is required. On the other hand, victim service professionals need to have clear guidance concerning information that may be shared with victims and respect the boundaries established by the interagency council.

Members of the interagency council should understand that the protocol development process is based on the needs defined by the Community Needs Assessment (Step 3 in the Protocol Development Cycle). Consensus about the community's needs facilitates the negotiations and expedites agreements about how to address these needs by the interagency council.

DOCUMENTATION

Protocol developed by the interagency council should use terminology that is understood by all participating agencies. One of the complicating factors with multidisciplinary efforts is that each discipline has its own "language." The protocol should recognize and overcome these language differences. Any terms that may have different meanings when used by different agencies should be operationally defined for the protocol. For example, *case* may have different meanings for each participating member of the interagency council. For law enforcement, *case* may mean a collection of related crimes consolidated into one investigation; for prosecution, it may mean one trial; and for victim services, it may mean one victim. If used in the protocol, *case* needs to be defined (and documented) so that all participants have a common understanding of its use in that context.

GUIDELINES

Protocol developed by the interagency council should establish guidelines for each of the participating agencies' responses to crime and its victims. Each guideline should have a stated objective so that the individuals using it understand its intent and are able to apply the guideline in spirit as well as in substance.

The guidelines establish the parameters for the activity, including

- which agencies are responsible;

- what they are responsible for;

- when they are responsible; and

- how the activity is to be carried out.

These guidelines are the basis for developing expectations among the participating agencies on the interagency council, as well as for understanding how the interdisciplinary/multiagency victim-centered system operates.

ROLES

The roles of agencies participating on the interagency council may seem self-explanatory, that is, law enforcement officers investigate and arrest; prosecutors prepare cases and prosecute; medical personnel examine and treat victims and are responsible for forensic evidence collection; and victim service professionals offer services such as counseling and advocacy for victims' participatory rights. The traditional roles of agencies are valid in a traditional operating environment. In a multiagency context, these roles must be redefined to reflect the interagency interaction.

An "interdisciplinary dependency" exists in victim-centered investigations. The protocol developed by the interagency council formally identifies such interdisciplinary dependencies and assigns specific responsibilities for each agency's role in the context of a cooperative system. For example, in the case of sexual assault, victims may first report the crime to a rape crisis center counselor who, in turn, is responsible for immediately informing those victims of a number of options available, including medical services, police reports, and counseling. Figure 3.1, the Multidisciplinary Sexual Assault Response Diagram, demonstrates some of the complexities of the system that confront the victim of sexual assault. Without protocol, which guides each agency's interaction with the victim, and which also guides each agency's interactions with every other agency, it is extremely likely that the victim's needs will be overlooked.

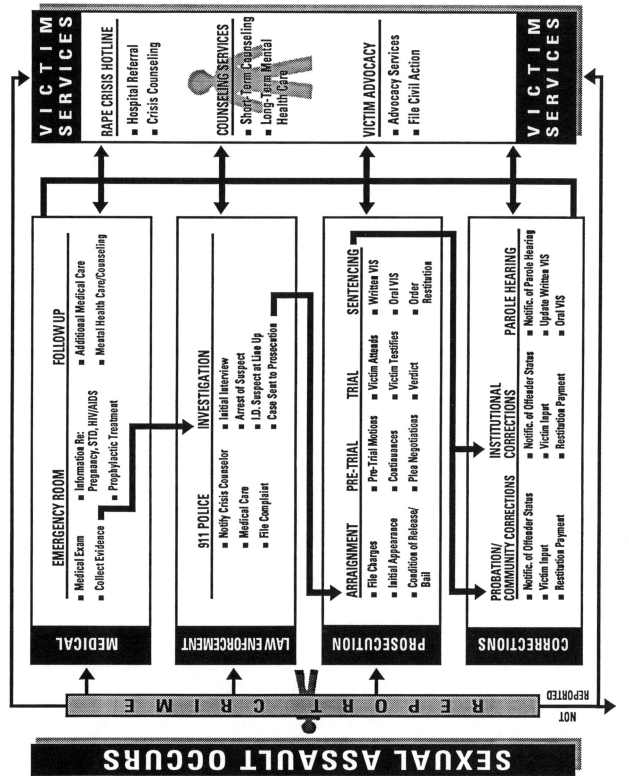

Figure 3.1. Multidisciplinary Sexual Assault Response Diagram

Protocol for Victim-Centered Systems

The interagency council has an opportunity to redefine the goals of the criminal justice system as it addresses the problems of crime in the community. Traditionally, these goals were defined in terms of number of arrests, cases closed, convictions, and so forth. These goals are perfectly valid but do not address the needs of crime victims. The protocol developed by the interagency council needs to have the following as an explicit goal:

increased attention to the needs of crime victims and their involvement in the decisions, which have an impact on them and the investigation, prosecution, and disposition of what, from their perspective, are *their* cases. (Patterson & Boles, 1992, chap. 2, p. 12)

In creating a victim-centered system, the interagency council needs to balance the needs of victims with legal requirements or other constraints of the criminal justice system. For example, victims of assault have serious concerns about their personal safety when their assailants are free in the community. It is not financially feasible for the police department to assign personal bodyguards to every victim; however, it may be possible to increase patrols in the victims' neighborhoods or to give these victims priority call status if they phone 911. Additional support may be available from victim service providers, thereby adding the dimension of interagency responsibility. This would assist crime victims in using the collective resources of several agencies, rather than being dependent on a single agency's resources.

Protocol Development Process

Development of the interagency council protocol is accomplished by members of the interagency council completing a series of eight steps. Each step in the protocol development process is sequential, with each succeeding step building on the products of the preceding steps. Using this approach, the interagency council is able to integrate its protocol with the resources available in the community. By following the eight-step process, the interagency council is also better able to address the needs of crime victims and the community. Because each interagency council tailors its protocol to the unique resources and needs of the community it serves, there are no model protocol that can simply be adopted and implemented by the interagency council.

The developmental process for the interagency council protocol consists of the following eight steps:

1. Inventory of Existing Services
2. Victim Experience Survey
3. Community Needs Assessment

4. Interdisciplinary/multiagency protocol writing
5. Formalized agency adoption of the protocol
6. Implementation training
7. System monitoring
8. Evaluation

These steps are described briefly in the following sections and in detail in Chapters 4 through 11. Protocol development is a cyclical process. The results of each completed cycle are considered during each succeeding cycle as represented in Figure 3.2.

Step 1: Inventory of Existing Services

This step requires the interagency council to develop listings of services available in its community that may be incorporated into its protocol for access by crime victims and their families, or by the members of the interagency council. The services to be listed include those provided by the members of the interagency council as well as other community-serving agencies and organizations. The Inventory of Existing Services can pave the way for a much broader cross-section of human and social service agencies or organizations becoming involved in a community's crime-fighting efforts.

The result of the Inventory of Existing Services is a directory of services, which should be distributed to all interagency council members as a ready referral reference. Each agency listing will have a contact name and referral criteria. A more detailed description of the Inventory of Existing Services is contained in Chapter 4. The results of the Inventory of Existing Services are also going to be used by the interagency council in subsequent steps of the Protocol Development Cycle.

Step 2: Victim Experience Survey[1]

The interagency council conducts a Victim Experience Survey (VES) designed to obtain an assessment of the criminal justice system from the crime victims' point of view. The VES should preserve the confidentiality of individual crime victim identities.

The interagency council should consider how it will include a sample of all crime victims in the VES, including those whose cases were dismissed before reaching court as well as those whose cases went to court but did not result in convictions. Each of the agencies and organizations providing services to crime victims should be included in the VES.

The VES, if administered prior to protocol implementation, can provide baseline data for evaluating the impact of interagency council protocol on crime victims when compared with results of VES performed after the protocol is implemented. The VES results are also included in subsequent protocol develop-

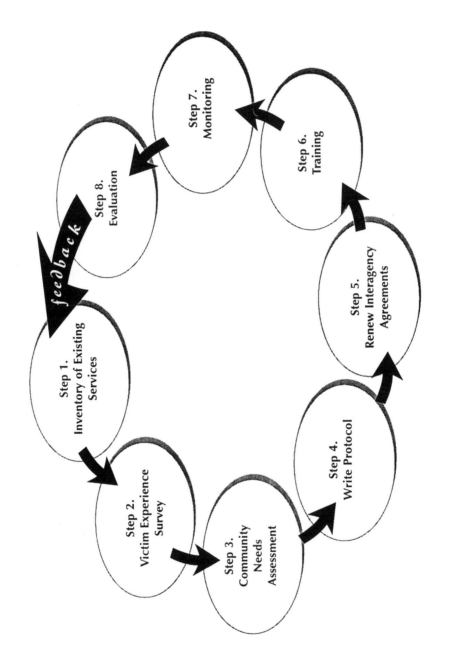

Figure 3.2. The Protocol Development Cycle

Step 1.
Inventory of Existing Services

Step 2.
Victim Experience Survey

Step 3.
Community Needs Assessment

Step 4.
Write Protocol

Step 5.
Renew Interagency Agreements

Step 6.
Training

Step 7.
Monitoring

Step 8.
Evaluation

feedback

ment steps. Detailed instructions for conducting the VES as well as a sample VES instrument are included in Chapter 5.

Step 3: Community Needs Assessment

As Figure 3.2 (diagram of the Protocol Development Cycle) illustrates, the results of the Inventory of Existing Services and VES are incorporated into the Community Needs Assessment. These results, however, are not the only information used to develop the Community Needs Assessment. Additional information needs to be gathered from the core agencies—law enforcement, prosecution, medical, and victim services—regarding the incidence of violent crime in the community, crime victim profiles, areas in the community most affected by crime, current responses to crime victims, and resource use.

We recommend that the interagency council convene a town meeting (in some communities, a series of public meetings) for the purpose of informing the community about violent crime and victimization and about the efforts of the interagency council to develop interdisciplinary/multiagency protocol. The town meetings should also provide an opportunity for members of the community to make their crime-related concerns known to the interagency council.

The interagency council should invite a broad spectrum of organizations, representing the diversity of population in the community, to send a spokesperson to testify at the town meeting. The interagency council should also invite organizations and individuals to submit written comments in lieu of testifying at the town meeting or to expand on their testimony.

All of the information from the Inventory of Existing Services, VES, town meetings, and agency service statistics must be processed by the interagency council. The interagency council should issue a Community Needs Assessment report describing how the system needs to be improved, specifically to meet the needs of crime victims. It should also address pertinent organizational and system issues. Detailed information about the Community Needs Assessment process and report is contained in Chapter 6.

Step 4: Writing the Protocol

The first three steps in the Protocol Development Cycle provide the foundation for the interagency council to write its protocol. In the first step, Inventory of Existing Services, the organizations or agencies that provide services to crime victims are identified. The second step, Victim Experience Survey, provides a constructive, but possibly critical, look at criminal justice system and social services agencies as they are currently perceived by crime victims. The third step, Community Needs Assessment, takes a broader look at crime and crime victims' issues in the community, providing an opportunity for information exchange between citizens, constituent organizations, and governmental entities.

The information from each of these steps is necessary for the interagency council to formalize its interdisciplinary, multiagency, victim-centered protocol.

The protocol should define the relationships between the organizations and address needs as indexed by the VES and Community Needs Assessment report. The interagency council may find that delegating the writing tasks to committees will facilitate protocol completion. The interagency council should review all protocol and reach consensus prior to submitting a final draft to the chief executives of participating agencies. Chapter 7 contains complete instructions for writing protocol.

Step 5: Renew Interagency Agreements

Once interagency council representatives agree on a set of protocol, each participating agency needs to have an opportunity to review and comment on the protocol and to formally adopt it as an operational guideline. The review and adoption process requires that the chief executive of each agency notify the interagency council when the protocol is accepted, and recommit to continuing to work with the interagency council during the implementation phase.

This is also a good time for the interagency council to consider expanding its membership to include other agencies or organizations that have a role in the implementation of the protocol. Chapter 8 provides additional details about renewing the interagency agreements and formal adoption of the protocol by participating agencies.

Step 6: Training

The interagency council should ensure that the protocol is implemented by developing a comprehensive training program for all personnel who have responsibilities covered by the protocol. To accomplish this task, an interagency council's *training committee* needs to conduct a Training Needs Assessment.

The Training Needs Assessment begins with analyzing each protocol provision and identifying the knowledge and skills necessary to implement it. As part of this assessment, all personnel responsible for implementing each protocol provision should be identified by position or name.

After developing the Training Needs Assessment, the interagency council develops a training curriculum and training schedule to ensure that individuals with protocol responsibilities have the requisite knowledge and skills. Chapter 9 contains more complete information about protocol-based training.

Step 7: Monitoring

To ensure that the protocol is being used, and to assess its effects on implementing agencies, criminal justice system personnel, and crime victims, the interagency council should establish a monitoring program. Monitoring implementation of protocol requires teams to observe the operations of participating agencies and organizations in situations requiring the use of protocol. Monitoring informs members of the interagency council about the implementation progress and enables them to make any necessary adjustments to ensure that the protocol is accomplishing its objectives without causing unanticipated problems.

The interagency council should create monitoring guidelines and develop formal reports for the organizations subjected to monitoring and for use by the interagency council. Chapter 10 contains more details about techniques for monitoring protocol implementation.

Step 8: Evaluation

Although monitoring is one form of evaluation, the interagency council should conduct a more rigorous evaluation of the effects the protocol has on system performance as well as on victim response. The evaluation should measure how well the protocol meets the following explicit objectives:

- Improve the crime victims' experience with criminal justice system agencies and other organizations.
- Maintain or improve the performance of criminal justice systems agencies as measured by traditional performance measures.

There are numerous texts that provide instructions for designing evaluations appropriate for use in evaluating the impact of protocol. This is not a textbook on evaluation; however, Chapter 11 contains a more thorough discussion of possible protocol evaluation techniques. Again, a formal evaluation report should be developed by the interagency council for use in revising the protocol (Patterson & Boles, 1992, chap. 2).

Planning and Feedback

At first glance, accomplishing the entire Protocol Development Cycle may seem daunting to the interagency council. To make the process more manageable, the cycle was divided into eight steps, each with distinct tasks that aid in their completion. An interagency council Task Schedule, as seen in Appendix A, was developed to help councils plan their work by designating who will accomplish each task and how long each task, step, and the entire cycle will take. By dividing the work into smaller segments, accomplishment of the eight steps becomes much more attainable.

It is important to note, however, that the development of the protocol is a cyclical process, with the results of each completed cycle used during the next cycle as the basis for making adjustments to the protocol. The duration of each cycle is determined by individual interagency councils; however, annual or biannual cycles ensure that protocol is kept up-to-date and responsive to changing community needs.

Chapter Summary

Whenever the word *protocol* is used in this text, it means: "The product of negotiations in which agreements are made and documented to create guidelines and assign roles for interagency council members" (Patterson & Boles, 1992, chap. 2, p. 8). This definition embodies several elements: product, negotiations, agreements, documentation, guidelines, and roles.

For protocol to be victim-centered, it must have as an explicit goal increased attention to the needs of crime victims and their involvement in the decisions that have an impact on them and the investigation, prosecution, and disposition of what, from their perspective, are *their* cases.

The development of protocol for the interagency council is an ongoing process. There may be a tendency, once the initial protocol is developed, to give a collective sigh of relief and consign the protocol to the bookshelf. It is important to resist that temptation. As explained in the following chapters, once protocol is developed, its implementation needs to be monitored and its effects need to be evaluated for the protocol to remain effective. In addition, developments in criminology, health sciences, law, and victim services dictate continually evolving protocol that maintains its legal and scientific relevance.

Note

1. In *Looking Back, Moving Forward: A Guidebook for Communities Responding to Sexual Assault*, the Victim Experience Survey was referred to as a Victim Satisfaction Survey. The Denver Sexual Assault Interagency Council changed the name to Victim/Survivor Experience Survey because it felt that "satisfaction" was the wrong type of measurement for a victim experiencing the criminal justice system. The authors of this book concur and modified the survey title to the Victim Experience Survey.

Reference

Patterson, J. C., & Boles, A. B. (1992). *Looking back, moving forward: A guidebook for communities responding to sexual assault.* (Available from the National Victim Center, 2111 Wilson Boulevard, Suite 300, Arlington, VA 22201)

CHAPTER 4

Inventory of Existing Services

Introduction

The first step in the Protocol Development Cycle is the Inventory of Existing Services. The purpose of taking inventory of the existing services is to examine areas in the community currently addressing violent crimes and to become aware of all services and resources available to crime victims. The inventory should be as comprehensive as possible, and it should include services from law enforcement agencies, prosecutors' offices, medical facilities, mental health programs, victim service organizations, and other social service organizations that are available to assist victims of violent crimes (Patterson & Boles, 1992, chap. 4, pp. 8-9).

The inventory should identify issues affecting service availability, accessibility, quantity, quality, and legitimacy (Koss & Harvey, 1991, p. 104). This information is obtained through a survey conducted by the interagency council. The result of the Inventory of Existing Services is a comprehensive directory of agencies and organizations providing services to crime victims within the community. Table 4.1 depicts the purpose, process, and product of the first step in the Protocol Development Cycle—Inventory of Existing Services.

Victim-Centered System—Responsibility Matrix

It may be easier to begin the inventory with the existing criminal justice system and create a map of current responsibilities for crime victims. One method of creating a picture of the current response system is to list the responsibilities of

TABLE 4.1 Step 1: Inventory of Existing Services

Purpose	Process	Product
To become aware of all resources currently being used to assist crime victims in the community	• Develop a master list of referral agencies and organizations • Conduct a survey • Develop a catalog of services	Directory of agencies and organizations that provide services to crime victims

each agency that has contact with crime victims throughout the criminal justice system. The Victim-Centered System—Responsibility Matrix (Appendix E), although developed as a planning tool for use by the interagency council in the protocol development process, can be used very effectively to identify levels of responsibilities attributed to criminal justice and community agencies that work with crime victims. The matrix also identifies areas in which agencies are working together on behalf of crime victims, and thus it provides an assessment of the current interagency efforts. Responsibility levels are denoted by a *P, S,* or *L* (Patterson & Boles, 1992, chap. 1, pp. 9-10):

P denotes a primary level of responsibility, meaning that the agency with a *P* in the agency column has the original, or principal responsibility. For example, law enforcement, as the first responder, is assigned the responsibility of determining if the crime victim is physically injured and in need of medical attention, thereby receiving a *P* in the police column for that item. If there is a shared responsibility—possibly the initial interview—the *P*s are given subscripts denoting the sequence of that responsibility, for example, P_1 in the police column and P_2 in the prosecutor's column, indicating a shared primary responsibility for that function.

S denotes a backup or secondary responsibility when it appears in an agency's column. For example, the prosecutor-based victim service provider may have the secondary responsibility of informing all crime victims of pretrial motions and hearings, thus receiving an *S* in the victim services column. The primary responsibility for this function may belong to the prosecutor, who receives a *P*.

L denotes a communications responsibility or linkage between the agency in whose column it appears and other agencies of the interagency council. For example, if a crime victim is admitted to a hospital emergency room, there may be a *P* under the medical column, with *L*s under the police and victim services columns to indicate the hospital's responsibility to notify police of the crime and ensure that the victim receives appropriate victim services—such as in a rape case in which physical trauma is often minimal but crisis intervention is essential. (The *L* designation may be more useful in the planning of interdisciplinary/multiagency protocol than in outlining the current system, as most jurisdictions have few formal linkages between agencies on behalf of crime victims.)

Figure 4.1 provides a brief example of how the Victim-Centered System—Responsibility Matrix can be used to create a current picture of the crime victim

VICTIM-CENTERED SYSTEM — RESPONSIBILITY MATRIX

KEY
P = Primary Responsibility
S = Secondary Responsibility
L = Communications Linkage

	Victim Services	Police	Prosecutor	Medical	Social Services	Mental Health	Schools	Courts	Probation/Parole/Corrections
RECEIVE VICTIM REPORT OF A CRIME									
911 / police department	L	P		L					
24-hour hotline	P	L		L					
Hospital emergency room	L	L		P					
Prosecutor's office	L	L	P						
FIRST RESPONDER									
Determine need for emergency medical care		P_1		P_2					
Arrange transportation to and from the hospital		S		P					
Determine if assailant is still nearby		P							

Figure 4.1. Victim-Centered System—Responsibility Matrix

61

responsibility system. Because responsibilities within the criminal justice system are not the same in every jurisdiction, this chart is for illustration purposes only.

When developing the Inventory of Existing Services, the interagency council should expand the example of the current victim response system by including other elements of the criminal justice system. These may include crime victims' compensation, investigation, arrest, arraignment/initial appearance, pretrial, plea negotiations, trial, sentencing, probation/community corrections/parole, and in-carceration.

Some interagency councils may also find it easier to divide victim responsibilities by specific crimes and complete separate matrixes for each crime. This recognizes that the criminal justice system may respond differently to various crime victims. For example, there may be more emphasis on responsibilities of medical personnel in rape cases as evidence is often collected in the hospital emergency room. In homicide cases, however, there may be less communication with family members of victims as these members may not have witnessed the crime. Keep in mind that this inventory reflects the current system, which may seem to be system-centered. By providing a complete picture of the current crime victim response system, the interagency council will be better able to identify areas that will help the system become more victim-centered.

Community Agencies and Organizations Serving Crime Victims

The Inventory of Existing Services also includes referral services for crime victims. It is important to collect information from all of the resources and services available to crime victims within the community for the following four reasons:

1. To determine if there are adequate services available for all crime victims in the community;
2. To ensure that the interdisciplinary/multiagency protocol accurately reflects the agencies and organizations available in the community to serve crime victims;
3. To ensure that programs serving all types of crime victims, including distinct victim populations, are included in the protocol; and
4. To provide a comprehensive list of quality referrals for victims of crimes.

To inventory services for all victims of crimes may be a very overwhelming task for interagency councils in some jurisdictions, particularly in larger, metropolitan areas, where populations are more diverse and service organizations are more plentiful. It may be helpful for the interagency council to create categories before beginning to tackle the full inventory. The purpose of the categories is to divide the information into more manageable segments. The categories can take on several forms, including the following:

Services:—such as crisis intervention, counseling/mental health, medical, emergency shelter, food and clothing, burial services, support groups, and so on.

Specific crimes:—such as homicide, rape and sexual assault, assault, burglary, family violence, and so on.

Distinct crime victim populations:—such as age-vulnerable victims, including child or elderly victims; victims who have disabilities, including those who are hearing impaired or deaf, visually impaired or blind, physically disabled or developmentally disabled; victims whose cultural, religious, or ethnic backgrounds may require specific accommodations including African Americans, Asians, Hispanics, American Indians, Pacific Islanders, or other ethnic groups; and those who have specific lifestyles, such as gay and lesbian victims, homeless victims, and so forth.

Geographic areas:—such as wards, quadrants, or other sections of a community; school and university campuses; Indian reservations; military bases; federal properties; and so on.

Once the interagency council has determined the categories for its inventory, its members should begin to create a master list of every agency or organization that exists in the community within each category. For each agency, the master list should include

Name of agency/organization
Name and title of contact person
Address
Telephone number
Fax number
E-mail address (Because more and more agencies are beginning to communicate by e-mail, requesting this address may enhance communications in some communities. Care, however, needs to be taken to preserve confidentiality of information and victims' privacy when relaying messages by e-mail.)

This preliminary master list will serve as the basis for a referral questionnaire. The interagency council needs to develop the questionnaire to identify the five critical issues listed in the chapter introduction: (a) service availability, (b) accessibility, (c) quantity, (d) quality, and (e) legitimacy (Koss & Harvey, 1991, pp. 104-107). The following section provides a list of questions that should be answered and a checklist of agency information that should be included in the questionnaire (Patterson & Boles, 1992, chap. 2, pp. 5-10). A sample of a referral questionnaire designed to address these five critical issues can be found in Appendix B.

The *service availability* section of the questionnaire should answer the following questions: What services exist? What qualifiers must be met in order for crime victims to receive services? Do criminal charges have to be filed? Do victims have to agree to testify at a trial? Is there a cost for the service?

____ Name of agency or organization
____ Identification of service(s) provided
____ Costs (if any)
____ Eligibility factors for service

The *accessibility* section should answer the following questions: Are services available in the times of greatest need or just during regular office hours? Are they located where crime victims can gain access to them? Do they have staff or volunteers that reflect the demographic make-up of the community, represent non-English speaking minorities, and offer wheelchair accessibility and provide service to those with other disabilities, and can they assist victims from different cultures?

____ Location(s)
____ Hours of operation
____ Proximity to public transportation (if available)
____ Compliance with American With Disabilities Act requirements
____ Languages or translation services available

The *quantity* section should answer the following question: Do enough services exist to meet the demand?

____ Case/work load
____ Existence of waiting list

The *quality* section should answer the following question: How good are the services that the community has available to crime victims? (Agencies need to make an internal assessment of their services, but they also need to use the Victim Experience Survey to cross-check their internal assessments. The interagency council should review the results of internal assessments and Victim Experience Surveys on a biannual or annual basis.)

____ Staff qualifications
____ Training
____ Feedback from clients

The *legitimacy* section should answer the following questions: Are the services that are purported to be available to crime victims really being provided? Do criminal justice agencies refer victims to nonprofit service providers? If the services are available and victims are not being referred, is it because the system agencies do not recognize the agency's legitimacy?

____ Referral sources (number of referrals from each source)

BOX 4.1

Sample Letter Informing Agencies and Organizations About the Protocol Development Process

Dear (name of contact person):

Recently, several agencies and organizations that provide services to crime victims formed the (name of community) Interagency Council. The purpose of the interagency council is to develop interdisciplinary, multiagency protocol for improving the response to crime victims within our community. The (name of organization) was identified by one or more members of the interagency council as either assisting an agency or receiving referrals from an agency to provide services to crime victims.

One of the initial steps in developing victim-centered protocol is performing a comprehensive Inventory of Existing Services in (name of community) that are resources for victims of crime. Your participation in this endeavor would be greatly appreciated. Please complete the enclosed form and mail or fax it to:

(Name)

(Address)

(City, State, & Zip)

(Fax number)

Your completed form would be most useful if received by (date due). Please indicate on your form if your organization would like to receive more information about the interagency council and its work or be notified about future meetings. If you have questions, please contact me at (telephone number).

Sincerely,
(Interagency Council Chairperson)

Each questionnaire should be mailed with a cover letter that explains the purpose of the interagency council and how the referral questionnaire will be used. Box 4.1 shows a sample letter that can be modified for use by interagency councils to inform agencies and organizations about the protocol development process and request that they complete and return the questionnaire (Patterson & Boles, 1992, chap. 2, p. 4).

Chapter Summary

The development of interdisciplinary, multiagency protocol to respond to the needs of crime victims depends on a systematic process—the Protocol Development Cycle—under the leadership of the interagency council. The first step in protocol development is the Inventory of Existing Services. This comprehensive inventory identifies, for council members, the current responsibilities for crime victims within the criminal justice system, as well as the community agencies and organizations that exist to provide services and resources to victims of crime. The collection of this information helps the interagency council to (a) determine if there are adequate services available for all crime victims in the community; (b) ensure that the victim-centered protocol accurately reflects the agencies and organizations available in the community to serve crime victims; (c) ensure that services representing distinct crime victim populations are included in the protocol; and (d) provide a comprehensive list of quality referrals for victims of violent crimes.

References

Koss, M. P., & Harvey, M. R. (1991). *The rape victim: Clinical and community interventions* (2nd ed.). Newbury Park, CA: Sage.

Patterson, J. C., & Boles, A. B. (1992). *Looking back, moving forward: A guidebook for communities responding to sexual assault.* (Available from the National Victim Center, 2111 Wilson Boulevard, Suite 300, Arlington, VA 22201)

CHAPTER 5

Victim Experience Survey

Introduction

The second step in the Protocol Development Cycle is the Victim Experience Survey (VES). This confidential survey is conducted to determine the victims' assessments of how well the system is responding to their needs. The VES should assess the feelings of crime victims regarding how their cases were handled and how they were treated by each agency. To find out information about how each agency responds to crime victims, it is important to capture crime victims throughout the criminal justice process, including those whose cases

- Are not reported to the authorities
- Are not pursued because the assailant is not apprehended
- Are not filed (or dropped) after the initial investigation
- Are not pled out and, therefore, do not go to trial
- Are not completed through trial but may or may not obtain a guilty verdict
- Result in a guilty verdict with sentences that may or may not include incarceration

It is obviously difficult and intrusive, as well as expensive, for each agency to survey crime victims; therefore, one agency from the interagency council should be responsible for conducting all of the surveys. The logical choices are law enforcement or victim service agencies. Both of these agencies are most likely to see victims when charges are not filed. By conducting the surveys at a specific time—such as 6 months after the crime occurs—the interagency council can obtain information from victims at different points in the system. Some interagency councils may elect to survey crime victims more than once, for example, surveying

TABLE 5.1 Step 2: Victim Experience Survey (VES)

Purpose	Process	Product
To obtain feedback from crime victims about their experiences with criminal justice system agencies and other service organizations	• Design the VES • Obtain permission from crime victims to send the survey • Send cover letter and VES • Tally the results	Information on crime victims' experiences with and feelings about their treatment by agencies and organizations with which they came in contact

the victim when he or she first enters the system, and then taking a second survey at a set interval of 6 to 9 months after the initial survey. This will measure victims' feelings of the system over time. It is important to remember, when designing and conducting the VES, that the primary emphasis should be placed on the *victims'* opinions and perceptions, not the *system's* goals (Patterson & Boles, 1992, chap. 4, pp. 9-10). Table 5.1 offers information about what will be explored further in the remaining sections of this chapter—the purpose, process, and product of the VES.

Privacy Considerations

When conducting the VES, the interagency council must address the concerns of many crime victims about maintaining the confidentiality of their identities. The VES does not require that victims identify themselves. It should be administered by members of the interagency council who have already been in contact with the victims, thereby keeping knowledge of the victims' identities limited to those already involved with the case.

The following list provides some guidelines for considering privacy issues and ensuring the confidentiality of those victims who are surveyed.

- At an appropriate time, ask crime victims if they would mind being contacted in the future for a survey about their feelings concerning the services they received.
- Design the VES instrument to permit confidential responses and identify the respondents only at their option.
- Prior to conducting the VES, contact the crime victims selected to participate to remind them about the survey and reassure them that their privacy will be maintained.
- Ask survey respondents where they would like to receive the form, that is, would they like the VES mailed to their home address or another address? Give them the option of picking up the form in person, as some may be concerned that another family member or colleague could inadvertently receive it.

- Make sure that any reports generated about the VES do not present information from which the identity of any single respondent could be derived.

- There may be media interest in the VES. Members of the media may want to interview crime victims about their experiences in the criminal justice system. This can be a constructive experience if the media representatives agree to respect the wishes of any victims who do not want their identities disclosed. Additional safeguards to follow include:

    1. Interagency council members facilitate contact with the media. Media is not given access to case files with names.
    2. All crime victims give consent (written, if possible) prior to being contacted by the media (Patterson & Boles, 1992, chap. 3, p. 2).

Selecting the Survey Sample

In some jurisdictions, it will be possible to survey every known crime victim or every victim of a felony. Larger jurisdictions may need to select a random sample of victims for the VES (or the initial VES if there will be follow-up surveys). Subsequent surveys, if conducted, will include all victims who were initially surveyed and who gave their permission to be resurveyed.

If it is not feasible to survey 100% of the crime victim population, then those victims who are surveyed *must* be selected on a random basis to obtain information that is reflective of the entire crime victim population. Randomization may be accomplished by several different methods. The following offers a few examples:

Lottery method—Cases are assigned sequential numbers and slips of paper with corresponding numbers are placed in a closed container and drawn. After each number is recorded, the slip of paper is placed back in the container so that the odds of being selected are maintained. For example, if there are 2,000 cases in the container, the odds of being selected are 2,000 to 1. If the slips of paper with the numbers are not placed back in the drum after being drawn and recorded, the next number would have odds of 1,999 to 1, the next 1,998 to 1, and so on.

Table of random numbers method—Many research methodology textbooks include tables of random numbers. The table used depends on the number of crime victims for the time period covered by the survey. For example, if there are between 100 and 999 crime victims, the table of random numbers would consist of 3-digit numbers. Any telephone directory can substitute for a statistics textbook. Open the directory to any page at random. Take the last two or three digits of the telephone numbers and match them to cases that are sequentially numbered (Patterson & Boles, 1992, chap. 3, p. 3).

Designing the Victim Experience Survey

The purpose of the VES is to determine how effective the system is at meeting victims' needs. Surprisingly, the VES is not widely used throughout the country. Thus, few examples of VES instruments exist. The one created for this text was designed on the premise that the best way to obtain system effectiveness information is by providing crime victims with a VES instrument and corresponding cover letter that is sensitive to crime victims' issues. When designing a VES instrument, the following characteristics should be considered. The VES

- collects information about all agencies and organizations that come in contact with crime victims;
- surveys crime victims who completed the criminal justice process, as well as those whose cases terminated prior to trial and court disposition;
- asks which services were offered and the level of satisfaction with each service;
- asks about other services crime victims would have found beneficial;
- asks about victim participation in case-related decisions and the level of satisfaction with that participation;
- provides an opportunity for crime victims to offer suggestions for system improvement;
- solicits the input of a diverse group of crime victims; and
- offers the option for victims to include identifying information for follow-up.

A sample VES is provided in Appendix C. It includes instructions for use, general and demographic information, and sections concerning law enforcement, prosecution, victim services, and medical services. The survey concludes by providing the victim with the option to reveal his or her identity for follow-up survey information (Patterson & Boles, 1992, chap. 3, pp. 5-11).

Conducting the Victim Experience Survey

Prior to sending out a VES, the crime victim should be contacted by the surveyor and asked to participate in the survey. This prior contact is an important form of empowerment for the victim and provides reassurance that the survey is legitimate and that confidentiality of the victim's case has not been compromised.

Surveys should be mailed to the address chosen by the crime victim, as some people prefer not to have case-related mail sent to their homes. Victims should also be given the option of picking up the survey in person.

Each survey packet should contain a cover letter, an addressed and stamped return envelope, and the survey instrument. The cover letter should reassure crime victims that their responses will remain confidential. A contact person should be included in the correspondence in case the crime victim experiences distress while

---

BOX 5.1

Sample Letter for Inclusion With the Victim Experience Survey (VES)

Dear (Ms. or Mr. Surname):

On behalf of the (name of community) Interagency Council, I would like to request your assistance in helping us improve our community's services for crime victims. You may recall that one of our staff members contacted you recently asking if you would mind responding to this survey. We appreciate that you expressed your willingness to complete the survey form enclosed.

The results of this survey will be used by all of the agencies of the interagency council to look for better ways to respond to the needs of crime victims. Your participation in this survey will enable us to more effectively assist individuals in the future who have shared experiences similar to yours.

We realize that some of the questions may cause you to recall difficult memories of your own case. If at any time the survey causes you to experience distress, please just return the form to us in the envelope provided and do not worry about completing the form. Also, you are encouraged to contact (name of crisis counselor) at (telephone number) with any questions or concerns you may have about the survey.

We wish to assure you that we will respect your privacy. The confidentiality of your responses is guaranteed. Again, your responses, along with those of all the crime victims participating in the survey, will be used to provide a comprehensive picture of how well we are meeting the needs of the victims, and will help ensure that future victims are spared additional trauma. Your completed survey would be most useful if received by (due date).

On behalf of the interagency council, I want to thank you again for taking the time to complete this survey.

Sincerely,
(Interagency Council Representative)

---

completing the survey and would like some assistance. If there is a deadline for response returns, indicate this date in the cover letter. Make sure that at least 2 weeks are allotted for participants to respond. See Box 5.1 for a sample cover letter for inclusion with the VES (Patterson & Boles, 1992, chap. 3, p. 4).

Chapter Summary

The second step in the Protocol Development Cycle is the Victim Experience Survey (VES). This survey provides interagency councils with information about the victims' assessments of how well the system is responding to their needs. When organizing and conducting the VES, the interagency council must take into account the privacy concerns of crime victims. Responses to the survey must be confidential and participants should be reassured of this.

To obtain information about how each agency responds to crime victims, survey participants must be representative of crime victims throughout the criminal justice system, including those who do not report the crime or whose cases are not filed. Participants should be selected on a random basis if it is not feasible to survey 100% of the crime victim population. Some methods of randomization include the lottery method and the table of random numbers method.

Finally, the instrument itself should include all agencies and organizations that come in contact with crime victims, provide a means to collect satisfaction information for all services, and offer the opportunity for respondents to suggest other services that might be beneficial. The primary emphasis should be placed on *victim* experience, not the goals of the *system*. When conducting the VES, the survey packet should be mailed to the address of each participant's choosing and include a cover letter and an addressed, stamped return envelope. Once the responses are returned and tabulated, the information will be used in the third step of the Protocol Development Cycle, the Community Needs Assessment.

Reference

Patterson, J. C., & Boles, A. B. (1992). *Looking back, moving forward: A guidebook for communities responding to sexual assault.* (Available from the National Victim Center, 2111 Wilson Boulevard, Suite 300, Arlington, VA 22201)

CHAPTER 6

Community Needs Assessment

Introduction

The third step in the Protocol Development Cycle is the Community Needs Assessment. This step is intended to answer two primary questions:

1. Based on the interagency council's information, what services does the community require to better meet the needs of crime victims?
2. What should the interagency council do to meet these needs? (Patterson & Boles, 1992, chap. 4, p. 10)

In addition to the Inventory of Existing Services and the Victim Experience Survey (VES), in this phase of the planning process, information should be sought from the community-at-large. A public hearing (or even a series of public hearings) provides an opportunity for each segment of the community to participate in the development of protocol. The exposure of violent crime and victimization as a community issue, and attempts to identify and meet the needs of crime victims, can begin to promote these critical questions as issues and involve the community in finding solutions. Public debate and exposure may also change victims' perceptions, thus enhancing both reporting of crimes and cooperation within the criminal justice system.

Finally, the Community Needs Assessment should culminate in the form of a report. This report should describe the way the current system operates, propose improvements to the existing system that address the identified needs, establish priority areas if all improvements cannot be made concurrently, and help frame provisions of the protocol by maintaining parts of the system that work and modifying those that need improvement (Patterson & Boles, 1994, p. 115). A comprehensive report that details the process for information collection, outlines the information obtained, summarizes the community's and crime victims' needs, and recommends changes that will provide the interagency council with a road-map for the protocol development process.

There are several tasks that should be completed when developing the Community Needs Assessment (see Figure 6.1). These tasks include the following:

1. Complete Inventory of Existing Services
2. Complete Victim Experience Survey
3. Appoint advisory committees
4. Conduct public hearings
5. Gather statistics on crime and victimization
6. Analyze collected data
7. Write Community Needs Assessment report

The first two tasks—Complete Inventory of Existing Services and Complete Victim Experience Survey—are addressed in the previous chapters (because these are large tasks that result in independent products, they are designated as separate steps in the Protocol Development Cycle). This chapter will address the other five steps for developing the Community Needs Assessment and producing a report.

Appoint Advisory Committees

The Inventory of Existing Services will help identify service providers within the community that are relevant to the needs of crime victims. The interagency council should invite these organizations to appoint a representative and to enter into the same written agreement as other member agencies. Individual membership on the interagency council, however, should be discouraged as it is difficult, if not impossible, to incorporate an individual into a system composed of agencies and organizations. Individual contributions are best made through participation on *advisory committees*.

The interagency council can benefit from the establishment of advisory committees for several reasons. Advisory committees

- provide council and support on issues pertaining to the interagency council's overall mission and specific objectives;
- provide knowledgeable experts and input, from both individuals and special interest groups that might not be included in the interagency council's regular membership, during the Community Needs Assessment as well as the protocol development and implementation stages; and

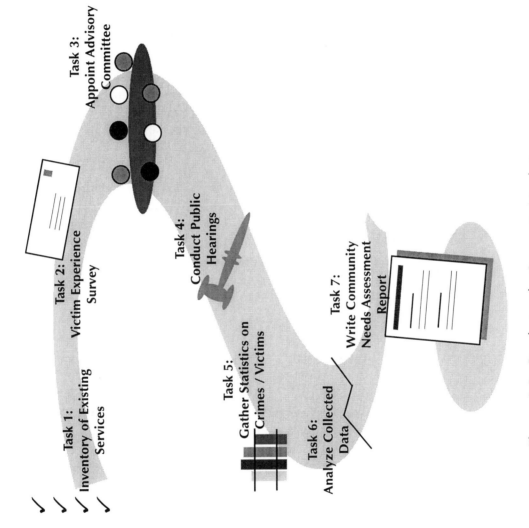

Task 1:
Inventory of Existing
Services

Task 2:
Victim Experience
Survey

Task 3:
Appoint Advisory
Committee

Task 4:
Conduct Public
Hearings

Task 5:
Gather Statistics on
Crimes / Victims

Task 6:
Analyze Collected
Data

Task 7:
Write Community
Needs Assessment
Report

Figure 6.1. Developing the Community Needs Assessment

- can review and make suggestions relevant to specific sections of the interagency council's protocol in which the advisory committee has expertise.

A variety of populations should be considered for the interagency council's advisory committees, including but not limited to crime victims, media, elected officials, and religious leaders (Patterson & Boles, 1992, chap. 9, pp. 10-11). Each of these groups of individuals represents critical elements in the treatment of and service delivery to crime victims, yet they are not likely to be associated with a member organization on the interagency council.

There are many roles that advisory committees can play in the development of the Community Needs Assessment. Crime victims on an advisory committee can help determine where, within the criminal justice system, the interagency council should be conducting Victim Experience Surveys. This committee can also review the survey and cover letter to ensure that they are victim sensitive. Finally, members of this committee may be good volunteer resources to help conduct the surveys and tabulate the results. A *media advisory committee* can support public hearings by printing the hearing announcements and through media coverage of the events. An advisory committee of elected officials can offer support and request the local crime statistics from appropriate sources, thus minimizing the "red tape" that often occurs during this process. Religious leaders may have good referral lists to offer for the Inventory of Existing Services. They can also provide testimony and promote participation in public hearings among their congregations and constituencies.

Regardless of the roles they play, each advisory committee should have a workable number of members (usually between 5 and 10 is sufficient). All advisory committees must have specific written responsibilities defining their roles in formulating the Community Needs Assessment, and reviewing and commenting on proposed protocol. The interagency council also provides written task assignments to advisory committees with deadlines for completing their work (Patterson & Boles, 1993, chap. 9, p. 2).

Conduct Public Hearings

A public hearing is an ideal forum for obtaining information and opinions from community members; however, it requires extensive planning to be successful. To ensure a broad spectrum of representation, notices should be sent to representatives from

- victim service agencies and mental health professionals;
- crime victim advocacy groups and networks;
- public agencies that assist crime victims;

- medical facilities and professional associations;
- ethic, religious, and cultural community centers and organizations;
- high school, college, and university student bodies;
- teachers, faculty, and administrators from all educational institutions including elementary level;
- elected officials and public policymakers; and
- other groups or individuals with interest in crime victim-related issues.

To receive maximum benefit from the public hearings, the interagency council should extend invitations to representatives of the groups and organizations listed above to testify. These representatives should speak for their constituencies, some of which may have distinct service-related needs, such as crime victims who are children or elderly, whereas others may be able to speak to the broader or more general issues of crime victim treatment within the criminal justice system. Individuals representing organizations should be encouraged to identify

1. successful aspects of the current service delivery system to crime victims;
2. barriers to effective delivery of services to their constituencies; and
3. services that organizations can provide to their crime victim constituents.

In addition, a public announcement of the hearing should be distributed to local media, organizations, churches, community centers, and so on, providing the general public with logistical information, such as time and place, as well as soliciting community members who wish to contribute information and testimony at the hearing. Box 6.1 contains an example of a public hearing announcement.

Members of the interagency council should also provide testimony concerning their perceptions of crime victims' needs. It is important that all individuals who testify be asked to provide a written copy of their testimony. A summary of the testimony from the hearings should be included in the Community Needs Assessment report.

Box 6.2 presents a checklist of what should be included in a public hearing agenda. A published agenda, which is distributed at the hearing, helps to keep presentations on track and offers information about what to expect from the hearing to speakers and audience participants.

The interagency council should request media coverage of hearings with the stipulation that media representatives respect the privacy of crime victims who testify. Media representatives should be briefed before the hearing and required to obtain written authorization from any crime victim they would like to highlight in their stories. Unless authorized by victims, reporters should withhold any identifying information and refrain from photographing crime victims in a manner that would reveal the victims' identities.

BOX 6.1

Sample Public Hearing Announcement

The (name of community) Interagency Council will hold a public hearing at (time) on (day of week and date) in (name of place and address). The purpose of the hearing is to obtain information about the needs of crime victims in the community. The interagency council will draw on this information as it develops interdisciplinary/multiagency protocol for responding to crime and its victims.

According to (name and title of official spokesperson), there were (number of) crimes reported in (name of community) last year. The actual number of crimes is unknown because, as documented in several research studies, many victims are reluctant to report the crimes committed against them. For example, over 80% of sexual assault victims are reluctant to seek help after their assaults and, therefore, do not make a report. Substantial underreporting also exists in domestic violence and child abuse cases.

Representatives of law enforcement, medical, religious, social services, victim services, and criminal justice system agencies, as well as several elected officials, are expected to testify during the hearing. Invitations were also extended to organizations serving distinct populations of elderly, disabled, and minority groups to speak on behalf of their constituencies.

Individuals who wish to present information at the hearing should contact (name) at (telephone number). Due to time constraints, speakers will be limited to five (5) minutes each in which to make their statements. Additional written information will be accepted by the interagency council.

Gather Statistics on Crime and Victimization

The Community Needs Assessment must examine the scope of the crime problem in the geographical area served by the interagency council. To document the nature of the crimes as well as the system's response to crime victims, the interagency council needs to collect and analyze data.

It is likely that most of the data needed for the Community Needs Assessment is being collected by local agencies in some form. Sources may include police crime reports, prosecutor case files, victim service organization statistics, and emergency room case counts.

There are many types of information that the interagency council should look for when collecting statistics. Some of the data specifications include but are not limited to

- Aggregate number of reported crimes for one year
- Number of crimes by type, such as homicide, rape, assault, and so on
- Number of crimes by type with age and sex of victim
- Number of crimes by time and days of week or month in which they occurred

---

BOX 6.2

Sample Public Hearing Agenda Checklist

Opening remarks, including explanation of the role of the interagency council and the purpose of the public hearing, presented by the chairperson of the interagency council.

General testimony concerning the nature of the crime and victimization problem in the community, presented by the chief of police or the district attorney.

Brief statements of need as identified by the core interagency council member organizations including law enforcement, prosecution, victim services, and medical team, presented by representatives of each member organization.

Statements by representatives of organizations receiving special invitations, with a list

of the organizations, and name and title of each representative.

Statements by representatives of other organizations or individuals making prior arrangements, with a list of speakers and their organizational affiliations (if any).

Open forum for others attending the meeting, with a 5 minute time limit for each speaker.

Invitation to submit written statements, presented by the chairperson of the interagency council.

Closing remarks and adjournment, presented by the chairperson of the interagency council.

- Geographic distribution of reported crimes
- Number of crimes reported to each agency, that is, law enforcement agency or victim service organization
- Number of cases at each entry and exit point in the system, that is, number of cases reported to law enforcement that were investigated and in which no further action was taken, number of cases investigated and sent to prosecutor, and so on
- Number of cases closed by arrest of perpetrator
- Number of convictions
- Average sentence and time served

If annual statistics are used, care should be taken to ensure that they cover the same 12-month period. Some agencies use a calendar year, while others may use a fiscal year (Patterson & Boles, 1993, chap. 4, pp. 4-7).

Analyze Collected Data

Complex statistical calculations are unnecessary for interpretation of the data collected for the Community Needs Assessment report. The interagency council needs to have data presented in ways that reveal strengths and weaknesses of the existing system and facilitate policy decisions. The following data presentation techniques should be considered when illustrating information in the Community Needs Assessment report.

Case studies—Data may be analyzed and a representative case developed that can be tracked through the system, with explanations of what typically occurs at each stage of the case. This case composite or compilation summary illustrates for the reader the process a victim is subjected to while involved in the criminal justice system.

Victim-based tracking system—The interagency council can create a flow chart of its system of response to crime victims. The number of victims, taken from case statistics, can be indicated at each point in the system to demonstrate how victims are processed through the response system and at what points in the system cases terminate.

Trend analysis—If data are available for several years (a minimum of 3 years), trends can be charted to determine if the problems are increasing, decreasing, or remaining stable over the time periods examined. Bar graphs or time lines may be good visuals to use when illustrating trends. The more years that data are available, the more accurate is the picture of trends in crime.

Victim profiles—Aggregating data on age, sex, ethnicity, and other demographic factors will develop a better understanding of the most prevalent profiles of victims for each type of crime addressed within the interagency council's protocol.

Offense mapping—Maps of the jurisdiction indicating the locations of crimes can identify patterns of certain offenses. It can also possibly identify areas that have characteristics that increase the risk of crime, for example, a subway stop with inadequate lighting that has a significant number of travelers after dark.

Pie charts—Graphically compare relative sizes (percentages) of the whole through wedge-shaped segments of a circle. These charts can be used to compare the

1. types of crime;
2. reporting of crime within each agency; and
3. percentage of crime within each segment (division, ward, quadrant, county, and so on) of the community (Patterson & Boles, 1993, chap. 4, p. 8).

All of these data interpretation techniques shed light on the current prevalence of crime and victimization. Simple illustrations included in the Community Needs Assessment report allow the reader to better understand the scope and nature of existing problems, which, in turn, can be used to help determine priority areas during protocol development for improving the system's response.

Write the Community Needs Assessment Report

At this point (after the Inventory of Existing Services, Victim Experience Survey, public hearings, and data collection and analysis), the interagency council is ready to write a report that describes the system as it currently functions and that identifies the specific needs to be addressed for improving the system's response to crime victims. The Community Needs Assessment report is a comprehensive examination of crime in the community. The following is a brief outline of the sections that should be included in the report.

Introduction—This section of the report identifies the agencies and organizations participating on the interagency council as well as the individuals that comprise the advisory committees. It also summarizes the processes used by the interagency council to develop the Community Needs Assessment and produce the report.

Community data on crime and victimization—This section defines the scope and nature of the current crime and victimization problem in the community. It should include aggregate numbers of reported crimes, agency-by-agency service statistics, crime victim information and profiles, and a description of the current response system for crime victims. Data interpretation techniques such as case studies, victim-based tracking systems, trends analysis, victim profiles, offense mapping, and pie charts can be used here to illustrate and clarify the information.

Inventory of Existing Services—This section offers a listing of all agencies and organizations serving crime victims, with a brief description of the services they provide. An appendix should provide more complete information about each of the agencies. In addition, a completed Victim-Centered System—Responsibility Matrix (as described in Chapter 4) further defines and illustrates the current response system and available services for crime victims.

Victim Experience Survey (VES)—This section presents the findings of the VES. Information from the survey should be organized by agency and system process. The information should present clear factors that indicate victims' opinions of the strengths and weaknesses of each agency's response to them, for example, 55% of respondents indicated that they were pleased with the response of the police 911 operator while 40% indicated problems and 15% had no opinion. In addition to numerical data, this section should discuss the factors related to response system strengths and weaknesses as indicated by the VES. The methodology for administering the VES should also be described.

Results from public hearings—This section presents the information derived from the public hearings. It should be presented in an organized digest format that highlights the key issues and concerns of those providing testimony. Footnotes may be used to indicate any sources of information from the hearings, and original written testimony can be offered in an appendix.

Findings of the interagency council—In this section, the interagency council should discuss its interpretation of the complete collection of information. It should include the strengths of the existing system as well as areas that need improvement, as the final protocol should preserve successful components while remedying those that are inadequate.

Priority concerns of the interagency council—This section presents the priority recommendations of what should be addressed in the protocol. These recommendations reflect the identified areas of the system that need improvement (Patterson

& Boles, 1993, chap. 4, pp. 9-10). They also begin to outline the methods of response to the identified needs on several different levels. These levels of response include the following:

1. Administrative: Administrative responses are those that are discretionary for the chief executive or director of each agency. Administrative responses may include changing procedures for case processing within the agency.
2. Budgetary: Budgetary responses include reallocating resources to address an identified problem, or seeking additional financial resources to increase service levels.
3. System: System responses reflect interagency functioning and "interfacing." A system response might entail redefining agency roles to more efficiently interact with crime victims, for example, the prosecutor may decide to contract with an outside victim service agency to provide victim assistance services rather than providing such services in-house.
4. Legislative: The interagency council may find that needs exist outside the scope of any agency's statutory authority, or that problems exist in the context of the criminal code defining a specific crime. The interagency council may decide to propose or encourage some specific legislative responses from other community entities, as well as inform and educate legislators of the need for remedial action.

These methods of response to the identified needs should be framed in the Community Needs Assessment report as areas to be considered when determining solutions and developing protocol. The report need not determine the appropriate level of response for each identified priority. This will probably take numerous conversations among the interagency council members and can be completed as part of the protocol development process. Rather, the report can recommend that the reported level of response be considered when developing protocol for each identified need.

It is important to note that at each level of response, the interagency council must consider a number of options or strategies for implementation. The task of the interagency council is to select the most reasonable course of action for the jurisdiction. These selection and implementation processes are not totally objective and may result in disagreements or conflicts among the constituent agencies on the interagency council.

An advantage of the interagency council is that each member agency may formulate *administrative* and *budgetary* responses in a *systems* context. This enables each agency to assess the impact of internal operational changes on the functioning of other participating entities. For example, would the creation of a special domestic violence unit in the police department have an impact on the prosecutor's office? How would the creation of such a unit affect the services of other agencies? How would it affect victims?

Better coordination of services for domestic violence victims, as in the previous example, may result in monetary savings to some agencies. A thorough examination of the community's needs, however, may result in the identification of important unmet needs for victims and, thus, the demand for additional funding.

Another advantage to the interagency council is the opportunity to present joint funding requests. Many governmental funding processes, either by design or default, pit agencies against each other in competition for funding. A similar interdisciplinary/multiagency coordinated effort in New Mexico resulted in a 25% net increase in state-level funding for children's programs in participating agencies (corrections, courts, social services, and mental health) at a time when the state was experiencing a decrease in overall revenue.

It is important to look at the Community Needs Assessment report as the launching pad for identifying needs, determining solutions, and developing protocol that reflects the solutions. This critical report examines the current crime and victimization problems, depicts the current system of response, and provides the interagency council with the information necessary to make decisions about areas needing improvements and about agency responsibilities for implementing improved responses.

Chapter Summary

The Community Needs Assessment is the third step in the Protocol Development Cycle. The purpose of this step is to provide the interagency council with comprehensive information about the needs of crime victims in the community. This is accomplished by using the information obtained in Steps 1 and 2, Inventory of Existing Services and the Victim Experience Survey, and expanding on this information. In Step 3, the interagency council should appoint advisory committees to assist with conducting public hearings, collecting local statistics on crime and victimization, analyzing the collected data, and writing a Community Needs Assessment report. Table 6.1 depicts the purpose, process, and product of this important step.

The report for Step 3 should describe how the system currently works and propose improvements to the existing system. Because it may be difficult to implement all of the recommended improvements concurrently, this report should establish priorities for the interagency council to consider. These priorities can be determined by identifying potential levels of response for each recommended improvement. These response levels include: (a) administrative, (b) budgetary, (c) system, and (d) legislative. Because it is the task of the interagency council to select the most reasonable course of action for the jurisdiction, these response levels help council members determine which strategy for implementation is most reasonable given the current circumstances and constraints at hand. This comprehensive

TABLE 6.1 Step 3: Community Needs Assessment

Purpose	Process	Product
To examine how well the existing system meets the needs of crime victims and identify any unmet needs	• Merge information from the Inventory of Existing Services and VES • Appoint advisory committees • Seek additional input from the public • Gather relevant statistics • Analyze data for gaps in services	Report to the community identifying the strengths and weaknesses in the way crime victims are treated within the criminal justice system and any improvements to be made by the interagency council

report provides the roadmap for the protocol development process and is used extensively in the next step, writing protocol.

References

Patterson, J. C., & Boles, A. B. (1992). *Looking back, moving forward: A guidebook for communities responding to sexual assault.* (Available from the National Victim Center, 2111 Wilson Boulevard, Suite 300, Arlington, VA 22201)

Patterson, J. C., & Boles, A. B. (1993). *Looking back, moving forward: A program for communities responding to sexual assault, workbook to accompany the guidebook.* (Available from the National Victim Center, 2111 Wilson Boulevard, Suite 300, Arlington, VA 22201)

Patterson, J. C., & Boles, A. B. (1994). *Looking back, moving forward: A program for communities responding to sexual assault, training guide.* (Available from the National Victim Center, 2111 Wilson Boulevard, Suite 300, Arlington, VA 22201)

CHAPTER 7

Writing Protocol

Introduction

The fourth step, and one of the most time-consuming in the Protocol Development Cycle, is writing the protocol. The purpose of writing interdisciplinary, multiagency protocol is to define, in writing, the roles and responsibilities of each agency as it responds to the needs of crime victims.

There are three stages for comprehensive protocol development. The first is to review the Community Needs Assessment report and confirm the methods of response (solutions) for improving each identified need. Once these are agreed on by the members of the interagency council, primary and secondary responsibilities, as well as communication linkages among agencies, need to be identified for each solution.

The second stage is to appoint a *committee of writers*. Writing protocol is an enormous task that is best handled by a team of contributors. The challenge of the interagency council is to determine writing assignments in a logical manner to ensure that each contributor is the most knowledgeable person available for his or her assignment. One person, however, should be responsible for the editing process to make sure that the protocol document maintains a single writing style and reads effectively.

The third stage of protocol development is the actual drafting of the protocol document. Organization is the key to this stage. The committee chairperson needs to determine realistic time lines based on the availability of the writers. Deadlines for drafts should be clearly articulated and adhered to. The final draft should be reviewed and approved, not only by the members of the interagency council but also by the chief executives or directors of each affected agency (see Table 7.1).

TABLE 7.1 Step 4: Write Protocol

Purpose	Process	Product
To develop written operational guidelines for all agencies working with crime victims which describe how the agencies will work with each other to assist crime victims	• Define protocol and reach a consensus on how the system should operate • Establish a committee of writers • Write protocol and review and approve drafts	Interdisciplinary, multiagency, victim-centered protocol

Stage One: Review the Community Needs Assessment

When reviewing the Community Needs Assessment, make sure that the levels of response or solutions to the identified needs are designed to create a victim-centered system. In creating a victim-centered system, the interagency council must balance the needs of crime victims with the legal requirements or other constraints of the criminal justice system. An important point that was made in Chapter 3 is that protocol developed by the interagency council needs to have as an explicit goal:

Increased attention to the needs of crime victims and their involvement in the decisions that affect them as well as the investigation, prosecution, and disposition of their cases. (Patterson & Boles, 1992, chap. 2, p. 12)

A Victim-Centered System—Responsibility Matrix, such as the one used in Chapter 4: Inventory of Existing Services to identify the way the criminal justice system currently functions, should now be used as a planning tool to identify potential roles and responsibilities for agencies that will address the identified needs. This form tracks the progress of a case through the criminal justice system and asks the interagency council to recognize victim-oriented concerns and determine, as a team, the most appropriate agency in the community to take the primary role in addressing each recognized concern. The interagency council also needs to identify agencies with a secondary role, that is, those that do not necessarily have a lead role in its resolution—rather, they may have a backup or secondary role to help ensure the system's success. Finally, the interagency council needs to determine if communication linkages are needed with other participating agencies. Although it may not be the primary or secondary role of an agency to address a specific crime victim need, that agency may still require an understanding of the circumstances surrounding the intervention so that it is better able to communicate with the victim and perform its job.

For example, one issue that may need to be addressed is the victim's choice to be notified of the status of an incarcerated offender. The solution to this may be to assign victim services the *primary* (P) responsibility for finding out if a victim wants to be notified of an offender's status, with prosecution having this as a *secondary* (S) responsibility. Prosecution then has the primary (P) responsibility for informing the corrections notification service of the victim's wishes. A *communications linkage* (L) is set up with victim services so that they are aware that the victim is registered for this service. This communication linkage may be accomplished through verbal contact, or perhaps a copy of the correspondence to the corrections notification service is forwarded by the prosecutor's office to victim services. This ensures that if a victim contacts victim services to discuss issues related to offender status notification, then victim services can immediately reassure the crime victim that he or she is registered with the service before determining the next course of action. These issues of organizational responsibility and communication linkages need to be addressed in the written protocol developed by the interagency council.

Stage Two: Appoint a Committee of Writers

Before drafting the protocol, the interagency council needs to first determine the general outline of the protocol, and then determine who will be the primary writers. It is important to outline the protocol before writers are selected because the outline may provide guidance for choosing the most appropriate writers. For example, if the protocol is divided into agency guidelines, it is best to select a writer from within each agency to represent that agency's interests. If the protocol is divided into stages within the criminal justice system, for example, pretrial, trial, posttrial, and so on, it may be more appropriate to establish a team of multidisciplinary writers to contribute to each stage. The challenge of the interagency council is to develop a protocol outline that is considered logical for the jurisdiction. Often an interdisciplinary approach is foreign to the current system, so the interagency council may adopt an outline that provides guidance for each agency and includes interdisciplinary/multiagency elements to help each agency with the transition to this new approach.

Once the outline is adopted by the interagency council, a committee of writers can be appointed. Criteria for selecting committee members include

- Clear understanding of the interagency council's goals and recommendations for change
- Knowledge of the protocol area to be drafted, that is, understanding of how a specific agency functions and the best procedures within that agency to implement proposed changes
- Time to be able to dedicate to protocol writing
- Skill in writing

Writers should also be members of the interagency council because they will have participated in the previous steps of the Protocol Development Cycle and decision-making processes. This will give them a strong foundation for writing the protocol. Outside writers are usually unable to articulate the intentions of the interagency council effectively.

An editor for the protocol also needs to be selected by the council. This person usually chairs the committee of writers. It is the responsibility of the chairperson to determine the format specification for the drafts. The chairperson should put specifications in writing and distribute them to the writers, as well as discuss these directions at a committee meeting. Similar draft formats will make it much easier to combine the drafts into one document.

The chairperson should also create a written time line for draft submissions. Protocol writing is a very time-consuming step in the Protocol Development Cycle and the schedule needs to be reasonable, given the other demands on the writers. The average time taken by interagency councils to complete this process is approximately 6 months. Once the schedule is set, every effort should be made to adhere to the schedule.

Finally, the chairperson offers the glue that adheres the drafts into one document through the editing process. The primary goal of editing is to mold the pieces into one style so that it sounds like a single document. The chairperson should not significantly change content without first discussing it with the writer. He or she, most likely, will not be well versed in the functioning of each agency. This is both an advantage and a disadvantage. If protocol is understood by the chairperson, it should also be clear to others who are not well versed in the operations of an agency. Significant changes by the chairperson during the editing process, however, may make it impossible for an agency to implement the new procedures.

Stage Three: Draft Protocol

Once the interagency council has identified primary and secondary responsibilities of individual agencies, discussed communication linkage requirements, and appointed a committee of writers, it is ready to begin drafting the protocol. The written protocol should identify the

1. Goals to be accomplished
2. Tasks necessary to achieve the goals
3. Procedures for carrying out specific tasks
4. Primary parties responsible for these tasks
5. Secondary or communication linkage roles, if any, other agencies will have (Patterson & Boles, 1992, chap. 4, p. 13)

One way to ensure that each writer includes all elements discussed and approved by the interagency council is to create checklists. Checklists should be organized according to the areas to be written by each contributor. If a writer is assigned all procedures related to a specific agency, then an agency responsibility checklist may be appropriate. See Box 7.1 for a sample checklist for the four primary agencies on the interagency council.

BOX 7.1

Sample Agency Responsibility Checklist

Protocol Checklist: Law Enforcement

Dispatcher

1. Determine if assailant is present.
2. Determine if emergency medical care is needed.
3. Dispatch patrol officer(s) according to department policy.
4. Determine if victim wants contact with victim services.
5. Keep victim on the line until patrol officer(s) arrive or transfer call to a victim services hotline operator.

First Responder

1. Reassure victim with appropriate language, such as "I am sorry this happened to you; it's not your fault; and you are safe now" (if this is true).
2. Determine need for medical care.
3. Arrange transportation to and from hospital.
4. Determine if suspected assailant is at the crime scene.
5. Ask victim for description/identification of assailant and broadcast be-on-the-lookout (BOLO) message regarding suspect.
6. Preserve the crime scene (if crime was recent).
7. Advise victim of availability of victim assistance and encourage acceptance of victim counseling and advocacy services.

Investigators

1. Keep victim informed about the status of the case.
2. Address victim's concerns for safety and the possibility that the assailant may return.
3. Accommodate victim's needs during investigatory processes that require victim participation, for example, interviews, hearings, and line-ups.
4. Notify victim when suspect is taken into custody.
5. Advise victim as to custody status of suspect and any changes in that status.
6. Permit victim advocate to be present during line-ups to provide emotional support for victim.

Initial Interview

1. Determine information needs for police *and* prosecutor from victim interviews to minimize necessity of repetitious interviews.
2. Provide appropriate steps to make victim comfortable with interview, that is, ask victim about gender preference of interviewer (especially in cases of sexual assault) or allow victim to have an advocate or friend present during interview.
3. Provide interpreter services if needed, including language translation for non-English speakers and signing for deaf victims.
4. Ask victim if he or she wants to file a complaint and have the case prosecuted.
5. If there is a stated policy about the use of videotaping, or audiotaping, or both, of the interview, inform victim of this process and how the tape will be used in later proceedings.

Protocol Checklist: Prosecution

General Prosecution Protocol

1. Notify victim of all hearings and changes in schedule.
2. Consider the needs of victim when scheduling case-related activities, for example, religious holidays, health requirements, family activities, and occupational requirements.
3. Facilitate victim participation in all activities at which the assailant has the right to be present, heard, or both.
4. Establish communication methods to avoid unnecessary trips to the courthouse, for example, electronic pagers, on-call system for victims, or voice mail system for victims to call in and receive current case status information.
5. Object to continuances unless they benefit the victim.

Initial Appearance, Arraignment, and Bail Hearings

1. Discuss desired conditions of release with victim prior to bail hearing.
2. Request that with any release, conditions include protection orders for the victim.
3. Keep victim informed about the detention status of the suspected assailant.
4. When possible, allow victim to express concerns about the suspected assailant's dangerousness.

BOX 7.1 (Continued)

Plea Negotiations

1. Inform victim of the reasons to consider a negotiated plea.
2. Describe optional courses of action other than the negotiated plea.
3. Determine what courses of action victim would like taken.
4. Consider victim needs when accepting a plea, for example, restitution, protection, emotional security.
5. Provide victim with the right of allocution at the plea hearing.

Trial

1. Provide separate waiting areas for victim and defense witnesses.
2. Provide court accompaniment service for victim.
3. Provide victim same access to the courtroom as afforded defendant.
4. Keep victim informed about court schedules: dates, times, and places.

Sentencing

1. Ensure opportunity for Victim Impact Statement as part of sentencing considerations.
2. Provide opportunity for a victim statement at the sentencing hearing.
3. Include victim needs as part of the sentence, for example, restitution, protection, emotional security.

Postsentencing

1. Notify victim about the changes in offender status.
2. Notify victim about scheduled parole hearings.
3. Ensure the opportunity for victim to update the Victim Impact Statement for the parole board.
4. Provide priority prosecution for violation of release conditions.

Protocol Checklist: Victim Services

Initial Report

1. Determine if victim is in immediate danger.
2. Ascertain if emergency medical assistance is needed.
3. Arrange transportation to and from the hospital.
4. Help identify and address the immediate concerns of victim.
5. Answer victim questions about law enforcement and the criminal justice system.

6. Offer crisis counseling and referral services.
7. Establish interagency coordination procedures.
8. Caution victim against evidence destruction (in applicable cases such as sexual assault).

Medical Examination

1. Provide victim with emotional support during the examination.
2. With victim's permission, discuss the crime with family and provide counseling and referral services for any secondary victims.
3. Guarantee that no victim has to leave the examination wearing only a hospital gown and sandals; arrange for replacement clothing.
4. Provide toiletries and cosmetics for use after the medical exam, forensic medical collection procedures, or both are completed.

Initial Interview

1. Establish guidelines for interagency participation in the interview.
2. Establish a clear understanding about the confidentiality of case-related information gained during the interview.
3. Define role(s) of the victim advocate during the interview, for example, provide emotional support, monitor attention to victim's needs, help inform victim about what to expect in the future.

Crime Victims' Compensation

1. Assign responsibility for assisting victim with completing the application for Crime Victims' Compensation.
2. Help follow-up on the application to ensure that it is processed in a timely manner.

Investigation

1. Establish procedures to facilitate communication between law enforcement investigators and victim.
2. Provide support for victim participation in the investigation.
3. Define procedures for easing fears about security and safety.

Arrest

1. Establish responsibility for notifying victim when an arrest is made.
2. Establish responsibility for notifying victim when there is a change in custody status of suspected assailant.

BOX 7.1 (Continued)

3. Provide guidelines for victim advocate's presence during police line-up and other proceedings.
4. Represent victim at hearings that are closed to victim's presence.

Pretrial

1. Establish procedures for notifying victim of case status.
2. Provide guidelines for coordinating communications among agencies providing other services to victim.
3. Develop court monitoring procedures and advocacy for appropriate victim participation in hearings.
4. Provide guidance for facilitating victim-prosecutor communications concerning plea negotiations and victim's needs.
5. Define the role of victim services in coordinating an "on-call" system for court appearances by victim.

Trial

1. Establish court accompaniment program by victim advocate.
2. Support the development of different waiting areas in the courthouse to completely separate victim from access by defendant and defense witnesses.
3. Furnish guidelines to offer ongoing emotional support to victim.

Sentencing

1. Define the role of the victim advocate for assisting victim with preparing Victim Impact Statement.
2. Support victim's right to allocution at the sentencing hearing.
3. Continue court accompaniment program.

Postsentencing

1. Remind victim of the right to seek redress through civil litigation.
2. Provide guidelines to keep victim informed about the status of appeals.
3. Establish procedures to keep victim informed about parole hearings and changes of incarceration status.
4. Help victim prepare or update a Victim Impact Statement for parole hearings.

5. Provide guidelines for enforcing restitution requirements and protection orders, and for reporting harassment.

Ongoing Victim Services

1. Provide guidelines for continuing services as long as victim requires emotional support or counseling.
2. Provide referral guidelines for other community services.

Protocol Checklist: Medical

Hospital Intake

1. Provide expedited consultation and attention to victim by specially trained staff.
2. In cases of sexual assault or where physical trauma is minimal, provide a private waiting area separate from the emergency room waiting area.
3. Establish procedures to obtain victim's consent for each medical and evidentiary procedure.
4. Provide guidelines for explaining to victim the significance of refusing an evidentiary examination—the right to refuse to file charges even if the evidentiary examination is conducted.
5. Define the role(s) of the victim advocate during the medical and evidentiary examination.

Evidentiary Examination

1. Conduct the examination in accordance with established evidence collection procedures, for example, rape evidentiary collection protocol.
2. Minimize the discomfort experienced by victim.
3. Directly handle evidence to maintain the chain of custody.

Medical Examination

1. Direct primary attention to the immediate needs of victim.
2. In the case of sexual assault, inform victim about possible pregnancy, sexually transmitted diseases, testing for HIV infection, AIDS, and prophylactic steps to avoid pregnancy and infection.
3. Provide guidelines for making referrals for follow-up medical and mental health services (Patterson & Boles, 1993, chap. 5, pp. 6-15).

Once the committee of writers completes its task of drafting the protocol and the initial drafts are edited to ensure consistent style, the protocol needs to be reviewed by the other members of the interagency council. An approval system by council members should be established. It is important that all members have the opportunity to see the protocol at this stage. Participation in this process will give all council members the knowledge and inspiration to promote the necessary changes during the implementation steps of the Protocol Development Cycle.

This may also be a good time to use the talents of the members of the advisory committees. Because advisory committees are comprised of individuals with specific interests or expertise such as victims, media, religious leaders, or public policymakers, if any protocol addresses areas within the specific expertise of advisory committee members, those members should be used to review the appropriate areas of the protocol and ensure its accuracy. Crime victims should critique the protocol to ensure that it is victim-centered and sensitive to the needs of victims.

Once the interagency council has completed the protocol review and approval processes, each participating agency must also be offered the same courtesy. The chief executive or director of each agency should be invited to review the protocol. This formal invitation should be written and offer a time frame for submitting comments. Because each agency will be implementing the protocol, the chief executive or director must be comfortable with the content. Once the person at the top of the organization has approved the protocol, he or she then issues the directive within the agency that provides the authorization to begin the implementation process.

It should be noted that a concern often mentioned by chief executives is the legal implications of a written approval of the protocol. Does this mean that the agency, its employees, or both will be held legally accountable for carrying out each responsibility as directed in the protocol? Will crime victims be able to sue if protocol is not carried out exactly as documented? These are legitimate concerns that each interagency council must tackle. On one hand, the council is developing the protocol to define roles and responsibilities to improve its response to crime victims. On the other hand, not all situations are the same and some may require a response that varies from the documented procedures. Rigidity may not be in the best interest of the crime victim, and professional judgment may be necessary to accomplish the desired outcome.

In 1994, the Snohomish County Task Force on Sexual Assault Protocols struggled with this challenge. The members of this Task Force selected to make a strong statement about their commitment to improving their response to sexual assault and prioritizing prevention of such crimes as their ultimate goal. They then added a disclaimer that reads, "These protocols are not intended to, do not, and may not be relied on to create any right or remedy, substantive or procedural, enforceable at law by any party in litigation with any person or agency associated with these protocols" (Snohomish County Task Force on Sexual Assault Protocols, 1994, p. 1-1). They go on to explain that the protocol represents "general operating guidelines" and that in some scenarios there may be more than one appropriate or necessary response for which "no protocol drafter can foresee all such contingencies." Finally, they felt it necessary to include that "these guidelines were not created to afford a criminal defendant any additional rights or procedural protections beyond those that exist by law, but to help effect a more *victim*-centered approach toward sexual assault crimes" (p. 1-2). Throughout their struggles to address this difficult challenge, they remained focused on the purpose of the protocol and committed to their implementation to affect positive change for sexual assault victims within the criminal justice system.

Chapter Summary

Writing the protocol is the fourth step in the Protocol Development Cycle. There are three stages to this step: (a) review the Community Needs Assessment, (b) appoint a committee of writers, and (c) draft the protocol.

It is important to review the Community Needs Assessment report prior to drafting protocol. This provides the opportunity for interagency council members to discuss the recommendations and clarify the solutions to the identified needs, as well as ensure that those solutions are defined in a manner that supports a victim-centered system.

Once there is a clear understanding of the intent and proposed content of the protocol, a committee of writers needs to be appointed. This committee should be chaired by the individual responsible for editing the document. The chairperson should also establish a specific format for the drafts and a time line for completion.

The final stage is drafting of the protocol. Checklists should be developed to ensure that all elements of the protocol are included in the drafts. The draft protocol should be reviewed and approved by members of the interagency council, and advisory committee members should be used to ensure that areas specific to their expertise are accurate. Once the interagency council agrees on the content of the protocol draft, the chief executives or directors of each agency should be offered the opportunity to review and approve the protocol. This provides them with the information needed to initiate protocol implementation and renew their commitment to the interdisciplinary/multiagency protocol that will enhance their response to crime victims. This commitment renewal is formalized in the next chapter, Chapter 8: Adopt Protocol and Renew Interagency Agreement.

References

Patterson, J. C., & Boles, A. B. (1992). *Looking back, moving forward: A guidebook for communities responding to sexual assault.* (Available from the National Victim Center, 2111 Wilson Boulevard, Suite 300, Arlington, VA 22201)

Patterson, J. C., & Boles, A. B. (1993). *Looking back, moving forward: A program for communities responding to sexual assault, workbook to accompany the guidebook.* (Available from the National Victim Center, 2111 Wilson Boulevard, Suite 300, Arlington, VA 22201)

Snohomish County Task Force on Sexual Assault Protocols. (1994). *Snohomish County's victim-centered protocols for responding to sexual assault.* (Available from the Snohomish County Prosecutor's Office, MS 504, 3000 Rockefeller, Everett, WA 98201)

CHAPTER 8

Adopt Protocol and Renew Interagency Agreement

Introduction

After the protocol is written, each agency affected should conduct an in-depth review culminating in an official response and eventual acceptance of the protocol document by its director or chief executive officer on behalf of the organization. This is also an excellent time to consider expanding the membership of the interagency council so that every agency or organization identified in the protocol has the opportunity to participate on the council. Table 8.1 depicts the purpose, process, and product of this essential step in the Protocol Development Cycle.

The following sections discuss the possible expansion of the interagency council and the protocol review and acceptance process.

Expansion of Interagency Council Membership

Additional agencies to be added to the interagency council (if not already members) may include:

- Social services (including Child Protective Services and Adult Protective Services)
- Mental health
- Schools, colleges, and universities
- Courts

TABLE 8.1 Step 5: Renew Interagency Agreement

Purpose	Process	Product
To obtain formal acceptance of the protocol by interagency council members and expand the interagency council, if necessary	• Interagency council members review and adopt protocol • Interagency Agreement is reviewed and amended • Interagency council issues invitations for new members	Renewal of the Interagency Agreement indicating acceptance of the protocol for implementation

- Corrections (including probation and parole agencies as well as institutional corrections)
- Organizations serving distinct populations (such as the homeless, crime victims with disabilities, or specific ethnic groups)

Each community has different agencies and organizations, as well as specific requirements for the effective implementation of its protocol. Based on protocol requirements, this may be a good point to consider expanding the interagency council (Patterson & Boles, 1993, chap. 6, p. 2).

INVITATION LETTER

The sample letter in Box 8.1 is for use by the chairperson of the interagency council when inviting additional organizations to join the council (Patterson & Boles, 1993, chap. 6, p. 3).

INTERAGENCY AGREEMENT

Box 8.2 is a sample Interagency Agreement. It was modeled after one that was used by the Child Sexual Abuse Investigation Team in Washoe County, Nevada. This agreement can be adapted to use at the inception of the interagency council for the initial protocol development commitment, or for this renewed commitment to protocol implementation.

At this point in the Protocol Development Cycle, it is important to obtain Interagency Agreements from any new organizations joining the effort. It is also important, however, to renew agreements with existing members so that all agencies are recommitted to the implementation of the newly developed protocol.

BOX 8.1

Sample Letter Inviting Additional Organizations to Join the Interagency Council

Dear (Ms. or Mr. Surname):

On behalf of the (name of community) Interagency Council, I am pleased to present this copy of the protocol adopted by the interagency council at our meeting on (date). It represents many hours of hard work by our members. The implementation of this protocol will ensure that the needs of crime victims in our community will be more sensitively and adequately addressed.

During the development process, members of the interagency council recognized the significance of your organization's services to crime victims, and we believe that the community would benefit from official representation of your agency on the interagency council. Your agency may join the interagency council by signing the enclosed Interagency Agreement. We also ask that you name an official agency representative to serve on the council. If you accept our invitation, please contact (name) at (telephone number) with the name of your appointee.

In addition, we are requesting that each of the agencies on the council review the protocol and formally incorporate its provisions into the individual agency policies. To document your acceptance of the protocol, I have enclosed a form for you to sign and return. Once all of the agencies have indicated their acceptance, we will develop training programs for all personnel affected by the protocol so that it may be implemented in an orderly and consistent manner.

Please do not hesitate to contact me if you have questions concerning the protocol or the activities of the interagency council. We appreciate the way in which your organization has assisted crime victims and hope that you will accept our invitation to become a member.

Thank you.

Sincerely,
(Name of chairperson)

Many interagency councils find that this is also an ideal time to notify the public of the council's progress by holding a formal ceremony for renewing member agency commitments to improving response to crime victims by adopting the protocol and approving its implementation. An Interagency Agreement signing ceremony, combined with a press conference, offers the chief executives or directors of the core agencies an opportunity to inform their constituents about the completion of the interdisciplinary/multiagency protocol and their commitment to implementing these new, victim-centered policies and procedures.

BOX 8.2

Sample Interagency Agreement

The participating entities herein share certain community goals and purposes in attempting to investigate, prosecute, and resolve criminal cases. Each participating agency and organization recognizes the requirement to address the needs of crime victims while fulfilling its mandated responsibilities. In combining our respective individual capabilities, each member agency seeks to increase the effectiveness with which such matters are dealt through the creation of the (name of community) Interagency Council, a communitywide, multidisciplinary, cooperative effort.

The purpose of the creation of the (name of community) Interagency Council is to provide and promote closer coordination and better communication among all participants herein. In addition, the community, the victim, and those otherwise involved in the matters of criminal cases will benefit from the guidelines and protocol to be established through cooperative assessment of the nature of the crime problems in this jurisdiction, the needs of crime victims, each agency's responsibilities, and the resources available to address these problems.

Each agency that associates with the (name of community) Interagency Council agrees to work toward the creation of standardized, victim-centered protocol for investigation, prosecution, and resolution of criminal cases. Each agency participating in this effort agrees to comply with the procedures set forth in the protocol.

Each agency associated with the (name of community) Interagency Council understands that it remains solely liable for the actions of its team members. Each agency agrees that there is no liability to the team by virtue of this agreement to informally provide public services.

Each agency that associates with (name of community) Interagency Council reserves the right to withdraw from the association. Each agency agrees that withdrawal will happen only after written notification to other team members.

Each agency whose representative signs this open letter of association does hereby commit itself to a cooperative effort to investigate, prosecute, and resolve criminal cases and assist crime victims.

(Provide signature blocks with date space for agency directors at end of Interagency Agreement)

TRANSMITTAL LETTER FOR INTERAGENCY COUNCIL PROTOCOL

The sample letter in Box 8.3 is for use when sending the interagency council's protocol to the chief executives or directors of the member agencies for review and ratification (Patterson & Boles, 1993, p. 4).

ADOPTION LETTER FROM AGENCIES

The letter in Box 8.4 is intended to be sent with the protocol to the chief executives or directors of the interagency council member organizations. It is to

BOX 8.3

Sample Transmittal Letter for Interagency Council Protocol

Dear (Ms. or Mr. Surname):

On behalf of the (name of community) Interagency Council, I am pleased to present this copy of the protocol adopted by the council at our meeting on (date). It represents many hours of hard work by our members, including (name) appointed from your agency. The implementation of this protocol will ensure that the needs of crime victims in our community will be more adequately addressed.

We are requesting that each of the agencies on the council review the protocol and formally incorporate its provisions into the individual agency's policies. To document your acceptance of the protocol, I have enclosed a form for you to sign and return. Once all of the agencies have indicated their acceptance of the protocol, we will develop training programs for all personnel affected so that the protocol may be implemented in an orderly and consistent manner.

Please do not hesitate to contact me if you have questions concerning the protocol or the activities of the interagency council. We appreciate your organization's able representation and participation in the activities of the council, and look forward to the implementation of this important protocol.

Thank you.

Sincerely,
(Name of chairperson)

BOX 8.4

Sample Adoption Letter From Agencies

Dear (Chair of Interagency Council):

I have reviewed the protocol developed by the members of (name of community) Interagency Council, which was presented to me on (date). (Agency's name) agrees with the protocol and is incorporating it into our policies and procedures. The implementation of this protocol will assist our staff in improving their interactions with crime victims. We look forward to participating in the training program and future activities of the interagency council.

Sincerely,
(Signature of agency chief executive) (Date)

be signed and returned to notify the chairperson that the protocol has been reviewed and adopted (Patterson & Boles, 1993, p. 5).

Chapter Summary

Providing an opportunity for the chief executives or directors of each agency to review and formally adopt the interagency council's protocol gives more assurance that there is genuine commitment by each organization to implement the protocol. Any questions or concerns held by member agencies will surface during this review process and require resolution by action of the full council.

The interagency council also needs to consider opening its membership to all organizations that have an identified role in protocol implementation. Broader membership on the council may facilitate communication among the participants in fulfilling the protocol requirements while enhancing community commitment to and services for crime victims.

Reference

Patterson, J. C., & Boles, A. B. (1993). *Looking back, moving forward: A program for communities responding to sexual assault, workbook to accompany the guidebook.* (Available from the National Victim Center, 2111 Wilson Boulevard, Suite 300, Arlington, VA 22201)

CHAPTER 9

Protocol-Based Training

Introduction

The interagency council should develop a protocol-based training program designed to accomplish two objectives:

1. To ensure that all personnel from each applicable agency and organization are aware of how the protocol affects each of their positions
2. To ensure that personnel affected by the protocol have the necessary expertise to carry out their responsibilities

To achieve these objectives, the training program may consume significant amounts of personnel resources from each participating agency or organization. For some agencies, virtually every position could be affected. For example, in law enforcement, all dispatchers, every patrol officer, and many investigators will probably need to receive protocol-based training.

The training curriculum should be interdisciplinary/multiagency, thereby reflecting the character of the protocol. Individuals from various agencies who are going to work together when using the protocol should begin their relationships by training together. This might mean that all "first responders" from law enforcement, crime victim hotlines, and medical facilities be trained together for that part of the protocol that addresses their specific roles. This mixture of personnel at training would change for other parts of the protocol based on the staff required for protocol implementation.

A major advantage of multiagency training is that it provides the opportunity to resolve role conflicts during the training and not in the middle of a case when the nature of the working relationship may be critical. Multidisciplinary teams are

TABLE 9.1 Step 6: Training

Purpose	Process	Product
To develop a protocol-based training program for all personnel affected by the interagency council's protocol	• Appoint a training committee • Conduct a Training Needs Analysis • Develop a training curriculum • Select instructors • Conduct a train-the-trainers seminar • Establish a training schedule	Quality training program that ensures that all personnel understand and are able to perform the duties required by the protocol

sometimes referred to as "uneasy alliances" (Pence & Wilson, 1994, p. 101) reflecting the stresses that can be present when disciplinary lines are crossed.

Developing a Protocol-Based Training Program

As Table 9.1 illustrates in the process column, there are several tasks that need to be accomplished to deliver quality training for protocol implementation. The six major tasks necessary for developing and delivering the protocol-based training include

1. Appointing a training committee
2. Conducting a protocol-based Training Needs Analysis
3. Developing a curriculum
4. Selecting instructors
5. Conducting a train-the-trainers seminar
6. Establishing a training schedule (Patterson & Boles, 1993, chap. 7, p. 1)

These tasks are explained in the following sections.

APPOINT A TRAINING COMMITTEE

The interagency council may decide to appoint a *training committee* comprised of personnel from each participating agency. Preferably, committee members should be individuals who have training responsibilities or expertise within their organizations. These individuals bring the training committee knowledge about their organizations' existing training programs, experience with curriculum design, and some familiarity with personnel who possess training skills.

The responsibilities of the training committee include the following tasks:

1. Conducting a Training Needs Analysis of the protocol
2. Developing a training curriculum for personnel responsible for implementing the protocol

   a. Survey agencies and organizations to determine the amount of time each is willing to commit to training
   b. Develop multiagency, joint training
   c. Consider phasing in the training so that time commitments by personnel are more easily integrated into their work schedules (For example, a 40-hour training program may be held one day per week for 5 weeks rather than on five consecutive days.)

3. Evaluating and certifying personnel knowledge and skills subsequent to the training
4. Selecting qualified trainers for conducting the training
5. Conducting an annual train-the-trainers course
6. Establishing a training schedule
7. Reviewing curriculum continually to ensure that it meets the requirements of the protocol and reflects the most current practices of victim assistance, case investigation, prosecution, and so on (Patterson and Boles, 1993, p. 2)

Delegating the responsibility for developing the training program to a committee permits the interagency council to continue its review of the protocol and not get tied up in the small details involved in training implementation. Creating the interdisciplinary/multiagency training curriculum, however, is a complex but extremely important step in the protocol development process.

CONDUCT A TRAINING NEEDS ANALYSIS

The training committee begins the process of developing the training curriculum by completing a Training Needs Analysis. The Training Needs Analysis links the processes specified in the protocol with the skills and knowledge needed to execute the protocol to the personnel who will carry out these processes.

The Training Needs Analysis should address the following issues:

- What training needs to be provided?
- Who (specific to each position in each agency) needs to receive training?
- How much training does each individual need?
- How should the training be evaluated?

The Training Needs Analysis Worksheet, in Appendix D, is designed to facilitate the analytic process. When using this worksheet, the training committee can list the caption or title for the relevant part of protocol in the first column.

The second column should list the position titles or, in some cases, the actual names of the individuals responsible for carrying out that piece of the protocol. For example, if the protocol describes dispatcher responsibilities for responding to crime victims, the individuals included in the training might be the police dispatcher, patrol officer, victim advocate, and police chaplain (or others identified that may be dispatched to a crime scene).

The third column should identify the knowledge required. Continuing with the previous example, the knowledge required for the dispatcher protocol would include understanding the psychology of victimization—how crime victims often react, resources available in the community to assist crime victims with distinct needs, familiarity with the state and local criminal laws, and protocol requirements.

The next column is for listing the skills necessary to implement the protocol. This is the "how to" column. Referring back to our example, the skills needed might include crisis counseling, first aid, investigative techniques, and implementing protocol procedures. Note: Even if all of the interdisciplinary team members are not involved in a particular procedure, they all need to understand what is happening and when it should happen.

The final column is for listing any materials that could support the implementation of the protocol. Returning to our hypothetical situation, these could include first aid kits, state and local criminal laws, evidence kits, and so forth.

Figure 9.1 illustrates the use of the Training Needs Analysis worksheet with the hypothetical situation previously described.

DEVELOP A CURRICULUM

After the training committee completes the Training Needs Analysis, it must develop the curriculum to meet these needs. This book is not a training curriculum development text. We do, however, offer the following suggestions:

1. The curriculum should have clearly stated objectives that are couched in behavioral terms. An example is, "At the end of this training session, the participants will be able to identify four characteristics common to victims of violent crimes."

2. The curriculum should use a variety of instructional techniques. Training to implement the protocol needs to include participatory teaching techniques as well as other teaching methods such as lectures and media-based instruction. Consider using technology-based instruction such as computer-assisted instruction and teleconferencing to reach hard-to-access audiences.

TRAINING NEEDS ANALYSIS WORKSHEET

Protocol / Guideline	Implementing Staff (Include Agency/Org.)	Knowledge Required	Skills Required	Support Materials
Dispatcher responsibilities	Police dispatcher,	Victim psychology,	Crisis counseling,	First aid kit,
	Patrol officer,	Community resources,	First aid,	State/local criminal law
	Victim advocate,	State/local laws,	Investigative techniques,	resources,
	Police chaplain	Dispatch protocol	Protocol implementation	Evidence kit

Figure 9.1. Training Needs Analysis Worksheet

3. The curriculum should specify how mastery of knowledge and skills will be measured and certified. Each module should include an evaluation scheme. Just as the techniques used to instruct participants in the training program should vary, so too should the feedback mechanisms. Evaluations could include observations of role playing, essay examinations, other paper-and-pencil tests, and supervisory on-the-job-training observation.

4. Just as the trainees are evaluated on their mastery of the curriculum, the curriculum should be evaluated by the trainees. This evaluation should be built into the design of the curriculum by the training committee.

Because individuals in different positions will need to have training specific to their responsibilities as identified in the protocol, the structure of the training is important. All personnel from each agency and organization affected by the protocol need to have a working understanding of the philosophical basis for the protocol—that it is *victim-centered*—and what that means for their positions. The training committee can organize the remainder of the training into modules based on the intended audiences for each module.

Victim advocates probably need to be included in each of the training sessions because they have victim-support roles throughout each stage of case handling. Other individuals may, at their own or their organization's option, participate in every training module. It is essential, however, that personnel specified by the protocol as having a role receive the specific training for their roles.

Once the training committee establishes the objectives for each training session, it should work with instructors to outline the content of the lesson plans, identify the instructional techniques, develop handouts and other support materials, and create the training evaluation instruments. The training committee should review and approve each lesson plan before incorporating it into the training curriculum.

SELECT INSTRUCTORS

The training committee should select trainers after it decides on the topics to incorporate into the curriculum. Trainers may be selected from experts employed by the interagency council member agencies and organizations, or the training committee may recruit outside trainers. The decision to use inside or outside trainers should be based on their qualifications, training skills, and the nature of the material to be covered. Often, trainers coming from the outside are perceived as neutral, without their own hidden agendas. Such individuals are useful to address conflicts such as "turf issues."

CONDUCT A TRAIN-THE-TRAINERS SEMINAR

The training committee needs to conduct a train-the-trainers seminar. The goals of this seminar are to

1. Acquaint the trainers with the victim-centered emphasis of the protocol-based training
2. Ensure that all trainers are competent in both subject matter and ability to impart skills and knowledge
3. Develop training skills so that the curriculum is presented to participants in a consistent manner

The train-the-trainers seminar should be repeated on an annual basis to train new trainers and to ensure that experienced trainers are kept up-to-date on the requirements of the protocol, new technology, and legal changes.

ESTABLISH A TRAINING SCHEDULE

The training committee's next task is to establish a training schedule that maximizes the opportunity for affected personnel to participate with a minimum disruption of their regular duties. This task is challenging, even under ideal conditions. In many cases, participating agencies will be faced with high caseloads, lack of funding, staff shortages, and other factors making it difficult to achieve the required commitment to training.

The training committee may accommodate personnel whose regular duties make it difficult to attend training over a number of consecutive days by scheduling the training series in short periods over several weeks. Another approach, for those who can accommodate a multiday training course, is to offer it on successive days. The training committee should consult the interagency council concerning how to best structure the delivery of the training to accommodate the needs of personnel receiving the training.

Chapter Summary

The training committee has two primary objectives: (a) to ensure that all personnel from each applicable agency and organization are aware of how the protocol affects each of their positions; and (b) to ensure that personnel affected by the protocol have the necessary expertise to carry out their responsibilities.

To accomplish these objectives, the training committee for the interagency council has several specific tasks that it must accomplish.

Training is an essential step of protocol implementation. Once the protocol training is completed, protocol implementation needs to be monitored. The next chapter offers information about monitoring strategies.

References

Patterson, J. C., & Boles, A. B. (1993). *Looking back, moving forward: A program for communities responding to sexual assault, workbook to accompany the guidebook.* (Available from the National Victim Center, 2111 Wilson Boulevard, Suite 300, Arlington, VA 22201)

Pence, D., & Wilson, C. (1994). *Team investigation of child sexual abuse: The uneasy alliance* (Interpersonal Violence: The Practice Series). Thousand Oaks, CA: Sage.

CHAPTER 10

Monitoring Protocol Implementation

Introduction

The interagency council has the responsibility of overseeing the implementation of its protocol. It, therefore, needs to determine a strategy for implementation and then initiates a mechanism for monitoring protocol implementation. This chapter outlines several potential implementation strategies and a monitoring program that will compare planned implementation objectives with actual achievements.

Monitoring is a diagnostic as well as an evaluative process. Monitoring questions how adequately the protocol works at the same time it seeks to identify specific problems that may hinder achieving optimum results. Because monitoring is closely related to the evaluation of protocol, the *monitoring committee* and the *evaluation committee* should work closely together.

Implementation Strategies

The specific strategy, or combinations of strategies, selected by the interagency council depends on the nature of the jurisdiction and the resources available. The interagency council should consider the following implementation strategies: pilot programs, systems phase-in, geographic implementation, and "just doing it" (Patterson & Boles, 1992, chap. 10, pp. 3-6). The council may also develop other implementation strategies appropriate to its jurisdictions. Whichever strategy is selected, however, it is the responsibility of the council to develop a step-by-step plan that identifies milestones and sets target dates for implementation of the full protocol.

PILOT PROGRAMS

Pilot programs enable the interagency council to field test protocol prior to full implementation by the participating agencies. The interagency council can adjust the protocol to address concerns that surface during the test period. Evaluation of the pilot program may be formal or informal. Regardless of the degree of formality used to evaluate results of the pilot program, the interagency council must articulate the goals of the protocol and criteria by which success of the pilot program will be measured.

Interagency councils should consider using pilot programs in large systems and when changes to the protocol are so complex that they may contain errors that need to be corrected prior to broader implementation.

SYSTEMS PHASE-IN

A systems phase-in strategy involves partitioning the response system into several components and implementing the protocol in one component before beginning to implement it in the next. This strategy is useful when the interagency council has a high level of confidence in its protocol but lacks the resources necessary for a system-wide personnel training program.

When using a systems phase-in strategy, the interagency council should establish a timetable or time-task line so that each organization is prepared to implement relevant protocol at a designated time. Without such a timetable or time-task line, organizational inertia may set in with its concomitant tendency to delay protocol implementation.

GEOGRAPHIC IMPLEMENTATION

As indicated by its title, geographic implementation is a strategy in which the jurisdiction is divided into sections and the interagency council implements the protocol in one section before initiating it in the next one. This strategy should be considered by interagency councils serving large geographic (possibly rural) areas. Geographic implementation, for example, enables the interagency council to train all personnel in a specific location at one time. As with the systems phase-in, the interagency council should establish a master implementation schedule for all geographic areas it serves.

"JUST DOING IT"

"Just doing it" is an implementation strategy with a comparatively high level of risk for the interagency council. This strategy may be appropriate in areas where participating organizations are accustomed to working together in interdisciplinary, multiagency endeavors, and for which the implementation of victim-centered protocol does not represent significant changes in responding to crime victims. The transition from system-centered to victim-centered responses may be abrupt. The "just doing it" strategy can disrupt the functions of participating agencies if the interagency council erred in formulating the protocol.

COMBINING IMPLEMENTATION STRATEGIES

Interagency councils may use combinations of strategies to implement protocol—for example, the protocol could be field tested in a particular segment of the response system using both the pilot program and systems phase-in strategies. The interagency council should select the implementation strategy, or combination of strategies, that will provide full implementation of the protocol within a reasonable time frame and with the least amount of disruption to services.

Monitoring Protocol Implementation

To identify the strengths and weaknesses of the protocol at each stage of the criminal justice process, the interagency council needs to address the following questions:

- Is the protocol being used by criminal justice system agencies and other community-serving organizations?

The interagency council should establish monitoring teams to make on-site visits to each agency for the purpose of determining the degree of protocol implementation. The monitoring team should also discuss the new protocol with personnel from the agencies visited to determine if there are operational problems with the protocol.

- For criminal justice system agencies that are fully implementing the victim-centered protocol, are there points in the process that seem to cause glitches?

Only after the interagency council has confirmed that victim-centered protocol is being implemented by relevant agencies at particular stages of the criminal process can it make inferences about the effectiveness of the protocol; effectiveness

TABLE 10.1 Step 7: Monitoring

Purpose	Process	Product
To determine the extent to which protocol is being implemented and to identify any problem areas in the protocol	• Appoint a monitoring committee • Initiate self-reports within each agency • Conduct site visits to observe the application of protocol • Inform the agencies and interagency council of protocol implementation progress	Reports on the degree to which the protocol are being used and what problems, if any, agencies are having with the protocol

is measured by Victim Experience Surveys, interviews or written surveys of agency personnel, and data about system performance.

The interagency council, during protocol implementation, should revise protocol based on findings from the monitoring process. Table 10.1 depicts the four primary monitoring tasks as the process in the monitoring step.

APPOINT A MONITORING COMMITTEE

The interagency council may delegate the responsibility of tracking protocol implementation to a monitoring committee. This committee helps the interagency council oversee the protocol implementation process. The monitoring committee's responsibilities are listed in Box 10.1.

Monitoring Tips

Monitoring protocol implementation should not be viewed as adversarial by individuals subject to monitoring. Monitoring is intended to ensure that, once protocol has been developed, it is being uniformly applied. Monitoring data are collected from reports submitted by the agencies implementing the protocol as well as from site visits made by monitoring teams. Both self-reporting and site visitation methods should be used by the monitoring committee (Patterson & Boles, 1993, chap. 8, p. 5).

SELF-REPORTING

Self-reports of progress toward full implementation of the interagency council protocol are prepared by each of the agencies and submitted to the monitoring

---

BOX 10.1

Monitoring Committee Responsibilities Checklist

The monitoring committee is responsible to the interagency council for the following tasks:

1. Recommending an implementation strategy to the interagency council—complete with target dates to provide the basis for monitoring progress

2. Maintaining a progress chart based on the time lines established by the interagency council

3. Assessing the degree of implementation of the protocol by each participating agency
4. Identifying roadblocks to implementing protocol
5. Assessing the impact of the protocol on victims
6. Assessing the impact of the protocol on participating agencies
7. Assigning monitoring teams for conducting on-site visits at agencies
8. Reporting findings to the interagency council (Patterson & Boles, 1993, chap. 8, p. 3)

---

committee for compilation and analysis. The monitoring committee communicates to the interagency council the progress reflected in these reports.

Self-reports are more effective when the monitoring committee develops a reporting form and provides it to each of the agencies and organizations after its approval by the interagency council. The format should be based on the implementation schedule adopted by the interagency council and the objectives established by the interagency council. To reduce the paperwork by the agencies implementing protocol, the report form should also capture information required to evaluate the impact of the protocol (as discussed in the next chapter).

SITE VISITS

Site visits by monitoring teams, usually carried out by personnel from agencies and organizations other than the one being monitored, is another method of providing oversight for protocol implementation. Team members interview agency staff, examine relevant records, and, if feasible, observe agency operations.

Monitoring teams can function more efficiently if members confer prior to the site visit to assign each team member specific functions for his or her monitoring visitation. For example, one member may be responsible for checking training records while another member interviews personnel.

Monitoring teams should schedule their visits in advance. On arrival, the team should meet with agency or organizational administrators to brief them about the purpose of the monitoring visit and meet with them again to debrief and to thank them for their cooperation.

Monitoring teams should write their report soon after their site visit so that their report accurately reflects the status of protocol implementation. The report due date should be included in the monitoring schedule established by the committee chairperson and submitted to the interagency council

Monitoring Tools

The monitoring committee may develop a reporting form for the agencies to complete and submit to the interagency council. The form should document progress made toward completion of the critical activities from the protocol implementation schedule. If there are any problems encountered with meeting the original schedule, the problems should be identified, a strategy for overcoming the difficulties explained, and the new target date set for achieving the goal.

The reporting form should also collect information concerning how well the objectives of the protocol are being fulfilled once the protocol is implemented. For example, if the objective was to reduce by 10% the number of trips crime victims have to make to the courthouse, the reporting form should capture that information. Any data required to evaluate the impact of the protocol should be collected and reported by the evaluation committee using the same reporting form as used for monitoring. Monitoring and evaluation data collection should be done as economically as possible so as not to burden the staff of participating agencies and organizations unnecessarily.

The Victim-Centered System—Responsibility Matrix, found in Appendix E, may be adapted as follows for use as a monitoring tool.

1. Take a blank matrix and identify the specific item of protocol in the first column.
2. Under the agency columns, indicate the agency responsible for implementing that specific protocol.
3. During a site visit to the agency, use the matrix as a checklist for protocol implementation.
4. On a separate piece of paper, or using a monitoring site visit reporting form, make notes regarding the findings of the monitoring team. (Patterson & Boles, 1993, chap. 8, p. 3).

Monitoring Report Guidelines

The monitoring committee is responsible for reporting its teams' findings to the interagency council and to the monitored agencies. The monitoring process is intended to assist with the implementation of the protocol for each of the agencies; therefore, it should not be viewed as adversarial.

As they perform their tasks, monitoring teams should look for strengths as well as weaknesses. The strengths should receive at least as much attention as the weaknesses in the monitoring report. When a monitoring team identifies a problem in the course of its duties, it should attempt to identify a probable cause and suggest solutions.

Prior to submitting its report to the interagency council, the monitoring committee should provide the agency with a draft of the applicable parts of the report, which will enable the agency to prepare a response. Again, monitoring is intended to be supportive of the agency's efforts and not intended to place the agency in a negative light (Patterson & Boles, 1993, chap. 8, p. 6).

Chapter Summary

Monitoring is an essential part of the protocol implementation process. Monitoring enables the interagency council to know how well the implementation process is progressing, whether there are problems, and the nature of any problems being experienced. This information is useful for keeping the project operating as intended.

Monitoring may be done through the collection of data reported from program sites or through actual observation of project activities by a monitoring team or a combination of both observing and reporting.

Monitoring is an important adjunct to evaluation as discussed in the next chapter. The monitoring process describes how well the implementation process is progressing. The evaluation process depends on the results of program monitoring to determine if any changes in system performance can be attributed to implementation of the interagency council protocol.

References

Patterson, J. C., & Boles, A. B. (1992). *Looking back, moving forward: A guidebook for communities responding to sexual assault.* (Available from the National Victim Center, 2111 Wilson Boulevard, Suite 300, Arlington, VA 22201)

Patterson, J. C., & Boles, A. B. (1993). *Looking back, moving forward: A program for communities responding to sexual assault, workbook to accompany the guidebook.* (Available from the National Victim Center, 2111 Wilson Boulevard, Suite 300, Arlington, VA 22201)

CHAPTER 11

Protocol Evaluation

Introduction

In the previous chapter, the monitoring process and its roles as both a diagnostic and an evaluative process were discussed. It was also noted that members of the interagency council who develop and implement the monitoring plan should work closely with individuals responsible for evaluating the effect of the protocol.

This chapter will review the eighth step in the Protocol Development Cycle, the evaluation process, and some of the issues the interagency council should address as it prepares to evaluate the protocol. It does not provide comprehensive evaluation information, only highlights of the basic evaluation concepts and some principal reasons for making the effort to perform an evaluation of the interagency council's protocol. There are many books available that provide detailed instructions for conducting an evaluation. Berk and Rossi (1990) include a helpful list of evaluation resources in the appendix of their book, *Thinking About Program Evaluation.*

Why Evaluate?

Evaluation is usually performed for one of three common reasons:

1. When a new program is initiated
2. When a funding source requires evaluation
3. When an organization wants to determine if it is meeting its stated objectives

TABLE 11.1 Step 8: Evaluation

Purpose	Process	Product
To determine the impact of the protocol on how crime victims are treated, as well as the impact of the protocol on the system	• Establish the evaluation committee • Design and implement the evaluation • Report to the interagency council	Report that examines the impact of the interagency council's protocol on crime victims and the performance of criminal justice system agencies

Unfortunately, evaluation seems to be a higher priority when major changes occur in established ways of operating than it is for existing services. The burden of proof is almost always placed on the innovative approach. Tradition is a powerful force for the status quo.

Encouraging the development of a routine evaluation system is the primary reason why we titled our eight-step process the Protocol Development *Cycle.* In a cyclical process, evaluation is a continuous part of the overall maintenance of the program. The system needs to change as victims' needs change, and the evaluation process can detect these changing needs and offer information that can guide protocol modifications. Thus, the primary purpose of the eighth step is to determine the impact of the interagency council's protocol on victim treatment and system performance. Table 11.1 offers an outline of the purpose, process, and product of the protocol evaluation. The rest of the chapter will focus on the process and product of this critical step in the Protocol Development Cycle.

The Evaluation Committee

The first stage of the evaluation process is to establish the *evaluation committee.* This committee is responsible to the interagency council for the following tasks:

- Developing and submitting to the interagency council, for its approval, an evaluation design to measure the impact of the interagency council's protocol
- Establishing data collection requirements and forms necessary to implement the evaluation design
- Overseeing the implementation of the evaluation design
- Using community resources, as appropriate, to carry out the responsibilities of this committee, for example, university faculty and students, private sector personnel and computers, and so on (Patterson & Boles, 1993, chap. 9, p. 2).
- Writing the evaluation report

Members of the evaluation committee should work closely with the monitoring committee because they may already have valuable information that should be included in the evaluation report. The interagency council may even find that a combined monitoring and evaluation committee is advantageous.

How Is Success Measured?

Presumably, at the time the interagency council was formed, the council's organizers sensed a need to combine forces and improve their response to victims of crime. That need should be verbalized and, if possible, quantified.

When interagency council members are fully engaged in the process of developing and implementing a new set of protocol, they may find it easy to lose sight of their original goals. For this reason, the interagency council should be clear about its objectives when it decides to evaluate its protocol—it should be specific about how it will determine success.

With both of the demonstration sites selected for the federal grant project, *Looking Back, Moving Forward,* the training team spent considerable time facilitating the development of mission statements to help the councils identify criteria for measuring success. Each of the interagency councils defined a mission statement specific to its own jurisdictional needs; mission statements are not generic and must be tailored to meet community priorities and interagency demands. For example, while one demonstration site's mission statement highlighted the need for interagency cooperation within the existing system, the other site focused its mission on transforming the current system to become more victim-centered.

Within each mission statement, there are words and concepts that need to be operationally defined (goals and objectives within the written protocol) and quantified (in measurable terms) to perform an evaluation of the success of the respective interagency councils. Thus, each interagency council must establish the criteria against which the attainment of the goals and objectives can be measured. Each criterion must be defined in measurable terms, which may include the following:

- *Time*—A process takes a measurable amount of time, such as fully implementing the protocol within 6 months from completion of protocol writing.
- *Quantity*—This measurement consists of counting something, such as increasing social service referral sources in the referral directory by 25.
- *Rate*—This measurement is made in terms of quantity per a designated amount of time, such as reducing prosecution-requested case continuances by 50% over the next year.
- *Quality*—This consists of subjective measurements of people's attitudes and opinions, which may be stated in terms of degrees of good or bad, or satisfactory or unsatisfactory, such as those used in the Victim Experience Survey.

It is important to formulate measurable objectives using *victim-centered* criteria versus the traditional criteria that are system-centered. Conviction rates, case clearance rates, recidivism rates, and case-load numbers or work hours all focus on the system, not the victim. Still, system information is important to collect, especially as it affects the victim. Examples of victim-centered criteria include the percentage of victims receiving victim advocacy services, number of personal contacts to inform victims of case progress, and an increase of positive victim experiences as measured by the Victim Experience Survey (Patterson & Boles, 1992, chap. 10, pp. 10-11). Because improved victim treatment will also improve the functioning of the system, victim-centered objectives will result in improvements within the system. An example of this is seen in the following objective—to reduce victims' fear of retaliation in domestic violence cases as measured by their willingness to testify—which was adapted from McKinney and Christensen (1979, pp. 37-64). Although the primary objective is to reduce victims' fear, obviously, cooperative victims will improve the functioning of the system.

HOW WILL THE EVALUATION BE USED?

The kind of evaluation the interagency council needs to perform depends, to a degree, on how the results of the evaluation will be used. This also relates to a parallel question, "Who will use the evaluation results?"

Evaluations should be planned with their users in mind. The users of the information extend beyond the members of the interagency council to include

- Legislative bodies, for funding and public policy considerations
- Representatives of the media, for informing the community about the effectiveness of the protocol development effort
- Leaders of other communities, to help decide if similar efforts should be initiated in their communities
- Professional and advocacy groups, for keeping informed about new developments in their respective fields

Very few administrators and policymakers find the technical language of statisticians very useful. Unless the evaluation is being completed purely as an academic exercise, evaluators must state their findings in understandable language and not attempt to be so technical and complex that their evaluation report is incomprehensible to their target audiences.

One evaluative measure is, "Did we do what we started out to do?" Merely answering this question may not be sufficient because, for example, increasing the assistance to crime victims may have created other unanticipated consequences. Although the interagency council may be most interested in the success of victim-centered elements of the protocol, decision makers and other users of the evaluation findings may need different types of information, including

- Cost comparisons—Does the protocol result in higher, lower, or the same operational costs?

- System effectiveness—What impact does the new protocol have on case closings by police, conviction rates by prosecutors, speedy trials, negotiated pleas, sentencing, and so forth?

- Victim attitudes—Do victims seem less traumatized by the actions specified by new protocol?

- Goal conflicts—Are there unintentional conflicts with mandated policy objectives caused by the new protocol?

The evaluation should be designed so that these issues can be examined and attributed to the changes in the protocol and not other factors.

ESTABLISHING A CAUSE-EFFECT RELATIONSHIP

Causality is a key element of program evaluation. The changes that are measured must be related to, or caused by, the changes in protocol and any alternative explanations must be identified and accounted for (Berk & Rossi, 1990, p. 101). For example, the implementation process for the interagency council's protocol specifies that all personnel should receive training to ensure that they possess the knowledge and skills necessary to implement the protocol. Unless there is a comparable training process in place for the existing operating procedures, improvement in performance could possibly be attributed to improved training and not implementation of the new protocol.

The use of *control groups* is one way to infer causality. If two groups that are otherwise similar are subjected to different processes, then it may be reasonable to conclude that any differences in performance are caused by the difference in processes. There are several ways to establish control groups. One of the most scientifically based techniques is to assign subjects randomly to each group—control and test.

With many programs, the random assignment of subjects to different groups is impractical so there is a need to create other comparison groups. If data already exist, the interagency council may be able to use a *before and after* comparison. In this kind of evaluation, the before group functions as the control group and the individuals who come into the system using the new protocol are the test group. To use this kind of evaluation, evaluators must be comfortable with the assumption that the individuals in the before group have the same or very similar characteristics as the individuals in the after group. Otherwise, the differences in evaluation measurements could be attributed to the differences in the individuals in the groups.

What Resources Are Available for Evaluation?

Evaluations can be very expensive to conduct. In addition to the expenses associated with designing the evaluation and devising data collection instruments, the cost of collecting data to evaluate protocol effectiveness may be quite high. These expenses must then be coupled with the expenses related to data entry, data analysis and interpretation, and final preparation and distribution of the evaluation report. The interagency council can lower some of the costs for evaluation by limiting the issues to be evaluated and restricting the data collection to what is necessary to measure the identified issues.

Some researchers have a tendency to collect too much data. They seem to feel that as long as data are being collected, everything should be documented "just in case" the researchers might need the data later. This is really a haphazard approach to performing the evaluation. A good evaluation design includes rigorously defined variables and well-thought-out calculations using carefully crafted data requirements.

A good place to start when establishing data requirements is with the data currently collected. For this reason, the evaluation committee should inquire at each agency to determine the existing record-keeping processes and information collection systems. The committee should collect copies of the blank forms currently in use to assess their usefulness for compiling data during the protocol evaluation process. The evaluation committee should also review the existing forms to see if any additional data requirements can be added, thereby reducing the number of forms necessary to collect information for use in the evaluation. A modification to an existing form may be more acceptable to the line staff than adding additional forms and increasing their load of paperwork.

The evaluation committee needs to know the extent that existing data are maintained in computerized databases. It may be feasible to extract the data elements needed for use in the evaluation from an existing database. If data can be obtained in this manner, the costs associated with processing these data will likely be much less than if the data were available only from original forms.

INSTRUCTIONS FOR COMPLETING THE
PROTOCOL EVALUATION WORKSHEET

In Appendix F, there is a worksheet that can be used by evaluators of interagency protocol. It provides a simple way of identifying the evaluation criteria to be used and where the data can be found.

Down the column on the left-hand side of the worksheet, the evaluation committee should identify the criteria to be used for the evaluation. In the next column, put either a "T" if the criteria are applicable to the test group or a "C" if applicable to the control group, and indicate with a "C/T" if they are applicable to both. In the third column, indicate the unit of measurement to be used. For example, a criterion could be listed as "time from offense to disposition." In the second column, the notation "C/T" would be entered because both control and test groups would use the information. The next column would list the unit of measurement as "days." In the fourth column, the source agency for the data is listed. The fifth and sixth columns call for a check mark if the data are extracted from an existing form or from a new form. The seventh column asks for the name of the individual who is responsible for completing the form. The final column is for comments regarding the criterion, units of measure, or the forms used for data collection. This column can also be used to indicate the frequency with which data are reported—weekly, monthly, quarterly, and so on, as seen in Figure 11.1.

Collecting and Analyzing Data

To the extent possible, data should be collected at or near the time of its generation. Trade-offs, however, may be needed based on practical issues. The interagency council may not, for example, be able to collect data from agencies' records on a daily or even weekly basis, so it should consider monthly or quarterly data reporting.

The data should be handled carefully to preserve its validity. Such careful handling may include

- Checking forms for completeness
- Maintaining files to ensure that no data are lost
- Checking all transferred information from its original documents to databases
- Double-checking all calculations

The interagency council will probably request interim evaluation reports from the evaluation committee. These reports should be progress reports on the evaluation and not reports of evaluative findings. If the interagency council reacts to interim evaluation reports and changes the protocol, the results of the evaluation may loose their validity because the processes used will have changed during the term of the evaluation. Therefore, it is important that the evaluation design include a specified length of time the evaluation process will take (usually a year).

The Evaluation Report

The evaluation report should be written with its users in mind. Box 11.1 shows an outline for a typical evaluation report.

PROTOCOL EVALUATION WORKSHEET

Criteria	C=Control T=Test	Unit of Measurement	Source Agency	Existing Form (✓)	New Form (✓)	Data Collector	Comment
Time from offense to disposition	C / T	Days	Prosecutor's office	✓		Victim / Witness Coordinator	Data collected monthly

Figure 11.1. Protocol Evaluation Worksheet

BOX 11.1

Sample Evaluation Report

I. Executive Summary

This is a brief statement of the findings and recommendations derived from the evaluation.

II. Project Description

This section establishes the basis for the evaluation. It describes the origins of the protocol development effort, the agencies involved, the problems that existed in the system prior to victim-centered protocol development, and the objectives for the protocol.

III. Evaluation Design

This section explains what was evaluated and how the evaluation was conducted. It should also explain why the particular design was selected, what data were used, and how the data were collected and analyzed.

IV. Evaluation Findings

This section presents the findings of the evaluation and explains what data exist to support each finding.

V. Recommendations

This section examines the findings and makes recommendations for adjusting protocol to better meet the needs of crime victims. Recommendations should also support continuation and strengthening of the positive findings documented by the evaluation.

VI. Appendixes

Include data collection instruments and other important documents that have facilitated the evaluation (Patterson & Boles, 1993, chap. 9, p. 6). Biographical information and credentials of evaluators may also be included here.

Chapter Summary

Evaluations should become a routine part of the operation of the interagency council and its use of interdisciplinary/multiagency protocol to improve services to crime victims. The evaluations need to be completed in accordance with existing methodological standards so that any changes in system performance can be attributed to the changes in protocol. Prior to carrying out the evaluation, the evaluation committee should check to see what types of data are already being collected, and if these data will be useful in evaluating the protocol. The worksheet in Appendix F will help the interagency council plan for and carry out its protocol evaluation.

The evaluation committee should also consider who the users of the evaluation will be and what kinds of information those users will find helpful for serving crime victims and in formulating decisions about the future of the interagency council. Although evaluation is a time-consuming process, the information derived from it is of the utmost importance. It indicates whether or not protocol is accomplishing established goals or if modifications are needed to improve services. It also tests whether or not protocol is being followed and helps ensure that written protocol remains active, because protocol that is relegated to a dusty shelf serves no purpose in transforming the system to be more sensitive to crime victim needs and maintaining a victim-centered approach to service delivery.

References

Berk, R. A., & Rossi, P. H. (1990). *Thinking about program evaluation.* Newbury Park, CA: Sage.

McKinney, J. L., & Christensen, D. L. (1979). *The evaluation plan workbook.* Cambridge, MA: Massachusetts Committee on Criminal Justice.

Patterson, J. C., & Boles, A. B. (1992). *Looking back, moving forward: A guidebook for communities responding to sexual assault.* (Available from the National Victim Center, 2111 Wilson Boulevard, Suite 300, Arlington, VA 22201)

Patterson, J. C., & Boles, A. B. (1993). *Looking back, moving forward: A program for communities responding to sexual assault, workbook to accompany guidebook.* (Available from the National Victim Center, 2111 Wilson Boulevard, Suite 300, Arlington, VA 22201)

CHAPTER 12

Continuing to Move Forward

Introduction

The future treatment of crime victims within the criminal justice system may very well determine the capacity of this system's ability to deter crime and hold perpetrators accountable for their offenses. The very fabric of our society may be threatened by the current cynicism regarding the criminal justice system. Yes, there have been improvements in the treatment of crime victims by criminal justice agencies as demonstrated by the passage of significant victims' rights legislation and the establishment of system-based victim service programs. There continue, however, to be areas for which progress needs to be made, and these areas contribute to the deteriorating confidence that society has in the criminal justice system. Creating and maintaining a system that treats crime victims with dignity and respect, and works to combat current cynicism that impacts our nation's ability to impart justice, is the mission of this book and the essence of the Protocol Development Cycle.

The job of the interagency council will not be completed when the first set of protocol is prepared and implemented. There will be a continuing need for the interagency council to address and resolve new challenges that constantly loom on the horizon. These challenges may be dictated by changing victim needs, enacting new legislation, advancing technology, or other influences of a changing society. To meet these challenges, the interagency council must continually obtain and process relevant information and be open to new roles that meet the needs of their community and the crime victims they serve.

Justice for Crime Victims—Still Needed

In the early 1980s, a presidentially appointed task force examined the treatment of victims of violent crimes by the criminal justice system. It would be ideal if substantial progress in the ways that crime victims are treated by the system could be itemized. True, some jurisdictions have made significant progress. The victims' rights amendments to several state constitutions and the creation of victim-witness assistance units in many prosecutors' offices should not be overlooked, but should be replicated as standard practice toward achieving justice for crime victims. Mandatory crime victim notification laws represent another important improvement made in some jurisdictions by requiring victims to be informed of scheduled parole hearings for their assailants.

There continues, however, to be many fronts on which progress needs to be made and too many crime victims still "fall through the cracks" in the system. A well-written, fully implemented interagency council protocol addressing the needs of crime victims can fill those cracks and ensure that victims of crime receive the information and services they need and deserve.

As an example of unmet victim needs, consider the recent case of a colleague who was sexually assaulted. This colleague is a victim advocate who does not say that her experience is representative of how rape victims are treated everywhere, or even of rape victims in the city in which she was raped. Her experience does, however, point to the need for improvements in the system so that no crime victim ever again has to endure similar treatment.

The details of the rape by the perpetrator are not relevant to this discussion and could breach the victim's privacy. It should be sufficient to say that the rape was at gunpoint and the victim felt her life was threatened. In addition to being raped, she was robbed of a small amount of cash and her credit cards.

After the rape, the victim reported it to the police. The reaction of the responding officer was disbelief that the rape occurred. One reason for the police officer's disbelief was his discovery of professional materials concerning sexual assault on the backseat of her car. The inference was that if you are a professional working with rape victims, you should not become a victim. The police officer also implied that the victim had read about rape so that she could concoct a believable story to report to the authorities.

In the process of the investigation, possible witnesses were told by the police that they doubted that rape had happened and that the victim was hysterical. Grudgingly they referred the rape victim to the emergency room of the hospital where she waited for two hours before a detective arrived with an evidence collection kit. The evidence collection kits were not available at the hospital due to the city's deteriorating financial condition.

The investigators finally accepted the notion that a rape had occurred when the assailant tried to use the victim's credit cards in a town about 40 miles from where the crime occurred. A short time later, a detective contacted the victim and asked her to appear at police headquarters for a scheduled line-up. She arrived at the appointed time only to be told by the detective that the line-up was rescheduled. It was the last time she heard from the detective. That was more than a year ago. Her attempts to obtain further case progress information have gone unanswered. She sums up her experience as having been raped twice—not only by the perpetrator but also by the system.

If an interagency council existed in the community in which this rape occurred, much of the distress suffered by this woman could have been avoided. Ideally, a victim service professional would immediately be available to assist a victim and would continue to help keep that victim informed of his or her case's status. In cases of rape or sexual assault, members of the community could help ensure that there were no more prolonged waits at the hospital due to lack of evidence kits, and police would be better trained to deal with these crime victims.

The Victim-Centered Approach—From Concept to Practice

The most important concept in this book is the need for communities to adopt a victim-centered approach. As we cited in Chapter 1, the research demonstrates that when victims' issues are addressed, the criminal justice system works better. Fears of increased case delays, fewer plea negotiations, case backlogs, and other system disruptions are groundless. Victims can, and should, be involved in decisions related to their victimization.

Although the system cannot heal victims from their crime-caused trauma, it can avoid causing victims further harm. This can be accomplished, in part, by merely affording crime victims normal human courtesies such as notifying them of hearing dates or any changes in scheduled times for hearings and other case-related processes, periodically reporting on case progress, providing information about the status of the suspected perpetrator, discussing decisions about plea negotiations, and providing crime victims an opportunity to address the court before the sentence is pronounced. Legislation enacted during the past decade in several states has codified these practices into legal rights for crime victims.

Creating a victim-centered system, however, should not be at the expense of the criminal justice system agencies whose responsibilities are often specified by law. As indicated in the earlier chapters of this book, the creation of an interagency council and set of protocol must balance the system's needs with those of crime victims to achieve justice.

The goals of the "system" are not in opposition to the goals of most crime victims. It is in everyone's interest—police, prosecutors, crime victims, and the community as a whole—to solve crimes, prosecute cases, and remove dangerous individuals from the community, as well as to treat victims in ways that foster their cooperation.

Outcomes From the Eight-Step Protocol Development Cycle

Each of the eight steps in the protocol development and implementation process provides the community with important information of value on its own merit. These are discussed here. It is, however, when the eight steps are completed that the full benefits of this process are realized.

The *Inventory of Existing Services* creates a database of all of the services available to crime victims. This offers the opportunity for criminal justice agencies and other organizations to make appropriate referrals and obtain services required by the crime victims they serve.

The *Victim Experience Survey* offers an opportunity for criminal justice agencies and victim service organizations to systematically receive feedback from clientele concerning the quality and adequacy of their services.

The *Community Needs Assessment* provides an opportunity for citizen participation in the process, thereby cultivating support for improvements to the criminal justice system. It allows criminal justice agencies and ancillary organizations to inform constituencies about problems within the system and proposed solutions for which support may be needed. It is also a feedback conduit from the community to the members of the interagency council.

Writing protocol documents the negotiated improvements for the system. When members of the interagency council write the protocol, it allows them to articulate and better define the roles and responsibilities between and among agencies. In addition, protocol constitutes an implicit contract, to which all can be held accountable for implementation.

Renewing the Interagency Agreement allows member agencies to recommit to the implementation of protocol after the protocol is reviewed and accepted. It also provides an ideal time to identify any additional agencies or organizations that would benefit the interagency council's efforts and invite these agencies to become members. Finally, it offers the opportunity to keep the community informed about the completion of the protocol and the initiation of implementation efforts through media coverage at a formal Interagency Agreement signing ceremony and press conference.

Training to implement the protocol offers each police officer, prosecutor, victim advocate, and any other personnel with a role defined in the protocol an opportunity to learn the skills and knowledge required to fulfill his or her specific responsibilities. Training is critical to the smooth implementation of the protocol. The resulting curriculum will benefit all of the participating agencies in strengthening their response to crime victims.

Monitoring the performance of criminal justice system agencies and victim service organizations provides their administrators with the opportunity to obtain information that can be the basis for many management decisions. Monitoring the implementation of protocol also provides information to the interagency council that enables its members to make decisions concerning the efficacy of the protocol as well as to determine the progress of its implementation.

Evaluation provides the interagency council with the opportunity to measure improvements in the system as well as detect new needs or problem areas that merit procedural changes and protocol revisions. This is an important, and often overlooked, element of protocol implementation. Unfortunately, evaluation is frequently reserved for use only with innovative or new approaches when it should be used even with traditional methods. The interagency council will need to schedule routine evaluations (biyearly or yearly) to determine the increment for improvements necessary to justify changing the operation of its criminal justice system.

This eight-step process enables the interagency council, public policymakers, and members of the community as a whole to better understand the resources necessary to help crime victims and the changes in the system that will enable the resources to be used efficiently and effectively for that purpose.

Protocol Development Cycle—Like Catching a Moving Train

For some communities, creating an interagency council and initiating this protocol development process will be like "catching a moving train." The criminal justice agencies in most jurisdictions may already have some protocol in place. Most likely, each agency has its own internal policies and procedures and many will not have to be changed to achieve a victim-centered response. The value of the eight-step Protocol Development Cycle described in this book is primarily in those areas in which one agency's operations interact with the operations of other agencies or organizations, and particularly those operations in which crime victims are involved or should be involved.

Regardless of how sophisticated the present system is, unless the agencies conduct a Community Needs Assessment, they lack the perspective necessary to identify needed changes in the criminal justice system. Criminal justice agencies also lose an opportunity to create a political constituency to support improvement of their services. This constituency may be very useful if the interagency council needs to seek additional funds from a governmental body. Many criminal justice system agencies appear to fear dialogue with the community. They seem to rely on introspection as a sufficient basis for evaluating their operations. Seeking outsiders' perspectives through the needs assessment and taking their input seriously are powerful steps toward developing broad support from diverse segments of the community.

Cooperation and mutual support to obtain resources for interagency operations are also strengths of this process. Many politicians who control the purse strings know that it is easier to deal with each agency individually when they are fighting each other for scarce resources than it is to deal with several who have united to present a set of priorities on which consensus has been developed and that have a broad base of support among the electorate.

Tangible Benefits for Working Together

An interagency council is not a panacea. There has to be true commitment for agencies to work together to achieve clearly articulated common goals. As part of the original federal grant project, *Looking Back, Moving Forward: A Program for*

Communities Responding to Sexual Assault, project personnel visited two cities and provided three days of training at each location.[1] Almost two years have passed since the trainings were conducted. We are pleased to report that both communities have made progress. Each has an established interagency council. One of the communities determined that there was a significant void in services addressing sexual assault. The interagency council in this community opened a child advocacy center to address problems of child abuse and child sexual assault. The police department assigned an additional officer trained to work with child sexual assault cases. The district attorney has developed a specialized unit to prosecute cases of sexual assault and has expanded its victim-witness assistance program. The other community already had specialized programs available for sexual assault victims, but reports that the interagency council helped improve communication and cooperation among member agencies, which, in turn, improved the quality of the services for these victims. Thus, each of these communities attributes its progress to the actions of the interagency council.

Putting together an interagency council to initiate the process presented in this book may seem like a daunting task. It does take time and resources. It does mean assessing current operations from top to bottom. It does require significant retraining of most personnel in all criminal justice system agencies as well as in community-serving organizations associated with the system. It will mean assigning additional responsibilities to personnel who may be already overtasked.

There may, however, be additional resources the interagency council can draw on. For example, both communities in the pilot program applied for, and received, state grants to hire staff to coordinate the interagency council's activities and to help write protocol. In the final analysis, however, creating the interagency council and faithfully conducting the eight steps in the Protocol Development Cycle presented in this book can be an investment that will pay significant dividends.

Future Challenges

Among the challenges to be faced in the future by the interagency council is developing ways to use emerging technologies to improve how crime victims are handled by criminal justice system personnel. The technology may be used to further depersonalize contact with crime victims or it may be used to strengthen personal contacts, to facilitate the exchange of information, and to increase the involvement of crime victims in the case decision-making process. Interagency council protocol addressing technological applications will ensure that such use of computers, cellular telephones, pagers, the Internet, and other emerging technologies will be planned with maximum benefit to the entire community.

As stated earlier in this chapter, newly enacted legislation or changing needs of crime victims may also create needs that indicate changes in the way criminal justice agencies function. Interagency councils should seek ways to remain in the mainstream of their communities so that they can keep themselves abreast of conditions that impact crime victims and that could lead to modifications in the ways criminal justice agencies do business. To do so, the interagency council may decide to expand its role in the community. Expanded council roles include but are not limited to the following.

Education—Members of the interagency council may decide that educating community members about the needs of crime victims, the implementation of the victim-centered protocol, or crime prevention strategies is paramount. Interactions during these education sessions with various community audiences, for example, students, business professionals, distinct populations, and so on, also help keep the interagency council in touch with the community.

Advocacy—The interagency council may determine that it can play a prominent role in influencing stronger laws for crime victims, as well as larger appropriations for government-funded victim services. Educating public policymakers as to the needs of crime victims and their service providers, as well as offering expertise in drafting appropriate legislative language, surveying constituents about victim-related issues, or just keeping policymakers abreast of new programs or victim-related activities in their jurisdictions, can contribute significantly to the advocacy efforts that ensure crime victims' rights and services.

Information repository—Rarely is there a group in a community whose role it is to research innovative programs and be a repository of information related to all areas of crime victims' rights, issues, and services. Often, each discipline collects information relevant to its role in the criminal justice process, for example, law enforcement may collect information on innovative investigative strategies or evidence collection procedures. An interdisciplinary/multiagency effort, such as the protocol development process of the interagency council, requires information that relates to all disciplines involved in the effort. In addition, each discipline benefits from a clearer understanding of the important developments related to other disciplines on the team. For these reasons, interagency councils may decide that it is important to collect and broker information to their members that will keep them abreast of new developments that impact the protocol and encourage a greater understanding of each discipline involved in the interdisciplinary efforts.

Key to interagency councils' success in keeping the protocol alive and viable is their ability to be flexible and determine which roles will enable them to remain in contact with their communities and abreast of the changes that affect the crime victims they serve. Because each community is unique, each interagency council will have to determine which methods are most effective given available resources. This is the council's opportunity to be creative in designing roles that will meet the challenges of an evolving society while using the talents and expertise of its members.

Actions Speak Louder Than Words

Today, the criminal justice system stands at a crossroad. Although the most recent crime statistics show that serious crime is declining, surveys continue to rank crime as one of the highest concerns of the American populace. These surveys indicate that a substantial portion of the population have lost faith in the ability of law enforcement and other justice agencies to represent the interests of everyday Americans.

To the extent that these agencies can convince the public that they are attentive to the needs of all citizens, the effectiveness of the criminal justice system will be enhanced. The eight-step process described in this book, the Protocol Development Cycle, is one way in which the system can communicate its concerns for the victims of crime.

Actions speak louder than words. When agencies unite to improve their capacities to help crime victims, that action becomes an audible message. When criminal justice agencies and victim service organizations develop protocol to help crime victims, that action becomes an announcement of concern. And, finally, when victim-centered protocol is implemented by well-trained professionals from members of the interagency council (an interdisciplinary/multiagency group), that action is like a crescendo of voices, speaking in unison and proclaiming for the entire community to hear, "We will succeed in bringing justice to everyone—including crime victims!" When this happens the entire community benefits.

Note

1. The authors believe that initial training to establish the interagency council's goals and objectives, and to build a cohesive, interdisciplinary group, provides a strong foundation for tackling the nuances of the Protocol Development Cycle. Feedback from the two pilot interagency councils has confirmed this belief. For more information about training, contact the authors at P.O. Box 3376, Alexandria, VA 22302. Copies of *Looking Back, Moving Forward: A Program for Communities Responding to Sexual Assault, Training Guide* are available from the National Victim Center, 2111 Wilson Boulevard, Suite 300, Arlington, VA 22201.

INTERAGENCY COUNCIL TASK SCHEDULE

Task	Target Date	Responsibility
Organization of the Interagency Council		
Appoint Interagency Council chair		
Develop committee descriptions		
Establish committees		
Appoint committee chairs		
Schedule committee meetings		
1. Inventory of Existing Services		
1.1 Create master list of organizations to be contacted		
1.2 Review referral questionnaire (Appendix B) and modify if necessary		
1.3 Conduct inventory		
1.4 Collect referral questionnaires		
1.5 Contact agencies and organizations that have not returned questionnaires		
1.6 Prepare inventory listing		
2. Victim Experience Survey (VES)		
2.1 Develop VES strategy		
2.2 Devise VES form (See Appendix C for sample form)		
2.3 Select survey respondents and make preliminary contact		
2.4 Send VES to crime victims who agree to participate		
2.5 Collect returned VES forms		
2.6 Tally results		
2.7 Prepare VES report		

Task	Target Date	Responsibility
3. Community Needs Assessment		
3.1 Collect crime and victimization data from appropriate agencies and organizations		
3.2 Schedule public meeting		
3.3 Invite officials		
3.4 Send media notices		
3.5 Set agenda		
3.6 Confirm attendance of officials		
3.7 Conduct public meeting		
3.8 Analyze information received from all sources		
3.9 Write Community Needs Assessment report		
4. Write Protocol		
4.1 Develop system concept - organization responsibilities		
4.2 Assign protocol writing responsibilities		
4.3 First draft completed and reviewed		
4.4 Second draft completed and reviewed		
4.5 Final draft completed and reviewed		
5. Renew Interagency Agreements, Expand Interagency Council		
5.1 Send protocol to every agency affected by their provisions to obtain sign-off on them		
5.2 Identify additional organizations that would benefit Interagency Council efforts		
5.3 Invite non-members to join the Interagency Council		
5.4 Review Interagency Agreement and revise, if necessary		
5.5 New Interagency Agreement signed by all Interagency Council members		

Task	Target Date	Responsibility
6. Training		
6.1 Appoint training committee		
6.2 Develop training committee responsibilities		
6.3 Conduct training needs analysis based upon protocol (see Appendix D for worksheet)		
6.4 Develop curriculum		
6.5 Identify trainers		
6.6 Conduct "Train the Trainers" program		
6.7 Schedule training		
6.8 Conduct training		
7. Monitoring		
7.1 Appoint monitoring committee		
7.2 Define committee responsibilities		
7.3 Develop monitoring checklists (See Appendix E for Responsibility Matrix form)		
7.4 Schedule site visits		
7.5 Draft reports		
7.6 Submit reports to the Interagency Council		
8. Evaluation		
8.1 Appoint evaluation committee		
8.2 Define committee responsibilities		
8.3 Develop evaluation design (see Appendix F for worksheet)		
8.4 Begin collecting data		
8.5 Submit interim progress reports to the Interagency Council		
8.6 Analyze data		
8.7 Write evaluation report with findings and recommendations for the Interagency Council		

INVENTORY OF EXISTING SERVICES REFERRAL QUESTIONNAIRE

1. Agency Information

Name of Agency

Name of Contact Person

Street Address

City   State   Zip

Telephone   Fax

E-mail

2. Services Provided

What primary services do you offer to, or on behalf of, crime victims?

_____ Counseling   _____ Support group   _____ Legal assistance

_____ Medical care   _____ Court advocacy/escort   _____ Referrals

_____ Other (Please specify)

What support services is your organization able to provide to crime victims?

_____ Emergency funds   _____ Child care   _____ On-call responses

_____ Lock replacement   _____ Transportation

_____ Other (Please specify)

3. Charges for Services

Does your organization charge victims for its services?

        Yes _____   No _____

If yes, what arrangements are available to assist clients with limited resources?

_____

_____

_____

4. Sources of Annual Revenue for Services Provided

Please indicate sources of revenue for services to crime victims and an approximate percentage of organizational income for each.

Federal government _____   United Way / CFC / Etc. _____

State and local government _____   Crime Victims' Compensation Fund _____

Individual contributions _____   Third party payments _____

Corporate contributions _____   Other (Please specify) _____

5. Field Offices / Branch Locations

Does your organization have field offices or branch locations?

Yes _____   No _____

If yes, how many of them serve crime victims? _____

Locations: *If necessary, please attach additional pages with addresses of field offices or branch locations, hours of operation of each, proximity to public transportation, accessibility to individuals with disabilities, and foreign languages or interpreter services.*

Location: _____

Hours of operation: _____ to _____

Number of blocks to public transportation:

Accessible to individuals with disabilities:

Yes _____   No _____

Languages: _____

Location: _____

Hours of operation: _____ to _____

Number of blocks to public transportation:

Accessible to individuals with disabilities:

Yes _____   No _____

Languages: _____

Location: _____

Hours of operation: _____ to _____

Number of blocks to public transportation:

Accessible to individuals with disabilities:

Yes _____   No _____

Languages: _____

Location: _____

Hours of operation: _____ to _____

Number of blocks to public Transportation:

Accessible to individuals with disabilities:

Yes _____   No _____

Languages: _____

6. Staff Information

How many paid staff provide services for, or on behalf of, crime victims? _____

Staff educational levels—indicate the number of staff in the boxes below reflecting their highest level of educational attainment.

☐ high school diploma   ☐ bachelor's degree   ☐ master's degree   ☐ post-graduate degree   ☐ other

Does your organization provide staff training?   Yes _____   No _____

If yes, please describe your training program below. Indicate topics and number of hours of training provided pertaining to crime victims and victim services.

Formal training for new staff:

_____

_____

Inservice training:

_____

_____

Specialized courses:

_____

_____

Provision for conference and seminar attendance:

_____

_____

Does your organization participate in training programs related to crime victims provided by other agencies or organizations?   Yes _____   No _____

If yes, please describe the training provided by other agencies or organizations:

_____

_____

_____

7. Volunteer Workers

Does your organization utilize volunteers?　　Yes _____　No _____

If yes, please give the job titles or functions for volunteer positions in your organization and the training requirements for each position.

Job title: _____　　Job title: _____

No. of volunteers: _____　　No. of volunteers: _____

Training requirements:　　　　　　　　Training requirements:

_____　　　　　　_____

_____　　　　　　_____

Job title: _____　　Job title: _____

No. of volunteers: _____　　No. of volunteers: _____

Training requirements:　　　　　　　　Training requirements:

_____　　　　　　_____

_____　　　　　　_____

8. Client Feedback and Evaluation of Services

Do you routinely survey crime victims about their satisfaction with the services provided by your organization or agency? Yes _____　No _____

If yes, please describe the process used to collect client feedback.

_____

_____

_____

_____

9. Referral Sources for Crime Victims

What are the sources of referrals of crime victims to your organization?

Source of Referral	No. of Referrals for 12 months From _____ to _____
Crime victims (self-referrals)	

This form was completed by:

_____　　　_____　_____
Name (Please print)　　　　　　　　　　　　Telephone　　　　Date

Instructions:

Our Interagency Council is conducting a survey of crime victims to evaluate their perception of the services they received after their victimization. The Interagency Council will use the information you provide to improve services offered to victims of crime. This is an anonymous survey and you need not give your name. You will be asked at the end of the survey if you would like to identify yourself for the purpose of participating in a follow-up survey. This is your option. All survey answers will be held in the strictest confidence.

The questions in the first section of the survey identify the initial agencies or organizations with which you had contact or which may have offered services to you. The following four sections ask about your satisfaction with the services you received from law enforcement agencies, prosecutor's office, victim assistance programs and medical services.

- *If you did not receive services from one or more of these agencies, please check the appropriate box for that section and proceed to the next section.*

- *If there are questions within each section that are not applicable to your experience, please check the "Not Applicable" box.*

Once you have completed the survey, please place it in the enclosed stamped, pre-addressed envelope and return it to the Interagency Council. The Interagency Council will compile the results of the survey without revealing the identities of the respondents.

If you experience emotional stress while completing the survey and would like to talk with a crisis counselor, please call the counselor listed below. If you are unable to complete the survey, please place the uncompleted survey in the enclosed envelope and return it to the Interagency Council.

Thank you for your help.

_____

Counselor/Contact Person   *Agency*   *Phone*

---

1. General Information

a. What was the first agency you were in contact with after you were victimized?

_____

_____

b. How soon after the crime did the contact with the agency or organization in the previous question occur?

_____

_____

c. Did the first agency contacted suggest that you should contact other agencies or organizations for additional assistance?   _____ Yes   _____ No

d. If you answered yes to the previous question, please list the agencies or organizations to which you were referred:

_____

_____

2. Demographic Information (For Statistical Purposes Only)

a. Date of Birth: _____ / _____ / _____   **b.** Gender: _____   **c.** Ethnicity: _____

d. Years of Education: ____High School   ____College   ____Grad, Post-Grad   ____Technical   ____Other

3. Law Enforcement / Police

The crime committed against me was reported to a law enforcement agency.

Yes _____   No _____

If no, continue to Section 4.

If yes, name of agency: _____

Please indicate your satisfaction with each item by placing an "X" in the appropriate column.

	Not Applicable	Very Satisfied	Satisfied	Neutral	Dissatisfied	Very Dissatisfied
a. Concern by the 911 operator for your safety.						
b. Timeliness of the response by patrol officers.						
c. Information given to you concerning what you might expect during the investigation.						
d. Sensitivity and professionalism of officers assigned to the case.						
e. Involving you in the decision making process related to the case.						
f. Accommodating your needs and schedule during the investigation.						
g. Referring you to community organizations that provide services to crime victims.						
h. Notifying you as soon as an arrest was made and the suspect was in custody.						
i. Addressing concerns about your personal safety while the suspect was not in custody.						

Comments on police involvement:

_____

_____

_____

_____

_____

_____

_____

_____

_____

_____

_____

_____

4. Prosecution

The crime committed against me was referred to the prosecutor's office.

Yes _____   No _____

If no, continue to Section 5.

If yes, name of office: _____

Please indicate your satisfaction with each item by placing an "X" in the appropriate column.

	Not Applicable	Very Satisfied	Satisfied	Neutral	Dissatisfied	Very Dissatisfied
a. Talking with you about the case and possible outcomes.						
b. Discussing the case with you prior to a decision not to prosecute.						
c. Demonstrating sensitivity and professionalism during interviews.						
d. Attempting to minimize court schedule delays.						
Plea negotiations						
e. Involving you in discussions related to plea agreements.						
f. Attempting to provide you the opportunity to address the court at the plea hearing.						
Trial						
g. Preparing you to testify in court.						
h. Accommodations while waiting to testify.						
Sentencing						
i. Assisting you to prepare a Victim Impact Statement.						
j. Attempting to obtain restitution for your losses due to the crime and your participation in the criminal justice system's investigation and prosecution.						
Post-sentencing						
k. Informing you about the custody status of the perpetrator after the sentence was imposed.						

Comments on prosecutor's office involvement:

_____

_____

_____

_____

_____

_____

_____

_____

_____

5. Victim Services Program

I received services from a victim services program.

Yes _____   No _____

If no, continue to Section 6.

If yes, name of program: _____

Please indicate your satisfaction with each item by placing an "X" in the appropriate column.

	Not Applicable	Very Satisfied	Satisfied	Neutral	Dissatisfied	Very Dissatisfied
a. Providing you emotional support to help you cope with the immediate crisis.						
b. Demonstrating a comprehensive knowledge about what you could expect from law enforcement and criminal justice system agencies.						
c. Assisting you in addressing your immediate concerns after the crime.						
d. Helping with family contacts and informing them of the crime.						
e. Obtaining your consent for services prior to delivery.						
f. Assisting you to complete an application for Crime Victims' Compensation.						
g. Facilitating communication with law enforcement and other criminal justice agencies concerning your case.						
h. Providing a victim advocate during interviews and medical examination (if any).						
i. Assisting with media inquiries concerning your victimization.						
j. Referring to other agencies for additional services.						

Comments on victim services:

_____

_____

_____

_____

_____

_____

_____

_____

_____

_____

_____

_____

_____

_____

_____

_____

6. Medical Services

I received services from a medical facility or emergency room.

Yes _____   No _____

If no, continue to Section 7.

If yes, name of facility: _____

Please indicate your satisfaction with each item by placing an "X" in the appropriate column.

	Not Applicable	Very Satisfied	Satisfied	Neutral	Dissatisfied	Very Dissatisfied
a. Accommodations while waiting for the examination to begin.						
b. Obtaining your consent *prior to* initiating examination procedures.						
c. Explaining the procedures to be used.						
d. Addressing your questions about the injuries or possible physical consequences of the victimization.						
e. Attempting to minimize your discomfort during the examination.						
f. Facilitating your examination after your arrival at the medical facility through prompt and uninterrupted attention by medical personnel.						
g. Informing you about sexually transmitted diseases, HIV/AIDS and possible pregnancy, if sexual assault.						
h. Demonstrating sensitivity to your needs as a crime victim.						
i. Providing facilities for washing after the examination was completed.						
j. Providing replacements for clothing taken as evidence.						
k. Furnishing transportation to and from the medical facility.						
l. Taking the financial responsibility for the examination and evidence collection, if sexual assault.						

Comments on medical services:

_____

_____

_____

_____

_____

_____

_____

_____

_____

_____

_____

7. Follow-up to this Survey

The Interagency Council would like to follow up with another survey in _____ months. If you would like to participate in this follow-up survey, please provide your name, address and telephone number where you prefer to be reached. All survey responses will be held in the strictest confidence.

_____
Name

_____
Street Address or Box Number

_____
City   State   Zip

Telephone: _____

Is this a day _____ or an evening _____ number? (Please indicate)

Again, thank you for completing this survey. Your responses will help us to improve services for crime victims.

TRAINING NEEDS ANALYSIS WORKSHEET				
Protocol / Guideline	Implementing Staff (Include Agency/Org.)	Knowledge Required	Skills Required	Support Materials

VICTIM-CENTERED SYSTEM — RESPONSIBILITY MATRIX

KEY
P = Primary Responsibility
S = Secondary Responsibility
L = Communications Linkage

	Victim Services	Police	Prosecutor	Medical	Social Services	Mental Health	Schools	Courts	Probation/ Parole/ Corrections

Appendix E

PROTOCOL EVALUATION WORKSHEET							
Criteria	C=Control T=Test	Unit of Measurement	Source Agency	Existing Form (✓)	New Form (✓)	Data Collector	Comment

Index

About the Authors

Anita B. Boles has more than 18 years of experience working with victims of violent crimes. In the late 1970s and early 1980s, she conducted training sessions on crisis counseling techniques for groups of volunteers working on local hotlines and at a rape crisis center in Kalamazoo, Michigan. She also developed counseling and education programs for students who were sexually assaulted on college campuses in Albany, New York. In 1984, she became Chief of the Victim/Witness Assistance Unit at the U.S. Attorney's Office in Washington, DC. Appointed to this position just after the release of the Attorney General's Guidelines for the landmark federal legislation—the Federal Victim and Witness Protection Act of 1982—she was challenged to develop a prosecutor-based program that met statutory requirements to become more responsive to victims and witnesses of violent crimes. In 1991, she received the prestigious U.S. Department of Justice Director's Award for her efforts. That year she also accepted the position of Assistant Executive Director of the National Victim Center to gain a national perspective on the plight of crime victims and to work on behalf of all of America's violent crime victims. During her tenure there, she directed a federal grant project in which she helped create an eight-step protocol development model to enhance community and criminal justice partnerships and improve response to victims of sexual crimes. The model became the basis for this book. For the past year, she has provided consultation services to a number of nonprofit and private organizations on proposal development and project implementation on a number of criminal justice grants and contracts related to violent crime and victimization. She has a bachelor's degree in social work and a master's degree in public administration.

John C. Patterson, Senior Program Director, Nonprofit Risk Management Center, has more than 25 years of significant experience in the nonprofit and government sectors. During his tenure in his present position, he has been the principal author of books addressing risk management issues related to abuse in community-serving organizations. He also provides consultation to several national organizations including the Boy Scouts of America, Special Olympics International, and the Civil Air Patrol. He is the principal author of *Looking Back, Moving Forward: A*

Guidebook for Communities Responding to Sexual Assault, which presents a process for the development and implementation of interdisciplinary, multiagency, victim-centered protocol. This project, conducted by the National Victim Center, was funded by the U.S. Department of Justice, Office for Victims of Crime. He has served as a consultant for several U.S. Department of Justice, Office of Juvenile Justice and Delinquency Prevention assignments including delivery of training and technical assistance to nonprofit missing and exploited children's organizations, and has authored materials on development of effective boards of directors, strategic planning, and fund raising. He was the principal consultant for designing the original Police Operations Leading to Improved Children and Youth Services (POLICY) training program for the Office of Juvenile Justice and Delinquency Prevention delivered at the Federal Law Enforcement Training Center, Glynco, Georgia. He also served on the staff of the National Center for Missing and Exploited Children and was the author of several of its publications. He has supervised programs in state and local governmental agencies as well as in community nonprofit organizations. He has delivered technical assistance and training in 36 states and in the District of Columbia.

NEED Help IMPROVING YOUR COMMUNITY'S RESPONSE TO CRIME VICTIMS' NEEDS?

TECHNICAL ASSISTANCE

CONSULTATION

Training is available.

The authors have developed a training program for communities interested in establishing an Interagency Council and following the eight-step *Protocol Development Cycle* model. The two and a half day training can be tailored to fit your community's needs. To request additional information, please fill out the form below and fax or mail it to:

Anita Boles and John Patterson
P.O. Box 3376
Alexandria, VA 22302
Fax: 703/684.9085

- -

Name and Title

Organization

Street Address or P.O. Box

City/State/Zip

Daytime Telephone   Fax

E-mail Address (optional)